SMS is determined to provide quality, ethical, and exciting adventures for the discerning hunter. Strang is a seasoned bowhunter with 30 years of experience in the field as a PH. Clients are welcome to hunt dangerous game and antelope with bow or rifle under his guidance.

Strang hunts in some of the best safari areas in Zambia with great success on lion, leopard, elephant, hippo, crocodile and buffalo, these being his main focus. Hunters may add on to their safaris on private land for unique Zambian plains-game species.

Camps, equipment and staff are all top-notch making our clients' safaris safe, comfortable and memorable.

Title: Lessons from an African Bowhunter
ISBN: 978-1-0370-1798-8
First Edition 2024
Contact: Strang Middleton
+260 977 826889 – text and WhatsApp
Email: strangm76@gmail.com

Lessons from an
AFRICAN
Bowhunter....

How to... and How Not to!

STRANG MIDDLETON
S A F A R I S

by Strang Middleton

INTRODUCTION

My bush days started when I was still in diapers, going on trips with my dad and grandfather doing anti-poaching in the Kafue National Park of Zambia, and hunting the surrounding concession areas. I still have a picture somewhere of me sitting on a buffalo's boss, being held by my grandfather, on my first buffalo hunt! My early introduction to hunting and wildlife management has proved invaluable to me. In turn, I have started my son Josh, at a young age too! I feel it is vital to teach our kids about the wonderful outdoors.

I know my love and knowledge of the bush came from this. While growing up I was always trapping, hunting with a sling shot, fishing and living off the wild. I would spend the whole day hunting and gathering, and my folks would not see me from dawn till dusk. We (my African friends and me) would only hunt, trap or catch and eat species that were edible, from insects to birds to snakes and even field mice... not to mention any other small mammal we came across. And imagine my mother's horror when at the age of six I manufactured a muzzle loader. One that worked I might add! After the first shot, she came flying out of the house and gave me the hiding I fully deserved, in the clearing powder smoke! I had learnt this trick from a poacher my father had caught some years back and turned into an "honest man" working on our tobacco farm and game ranch.

My love of the outdoors continued throughout my school years, and I excelled at falconry which taught me endless amounts about nature and the science that goes hand in hand with correct and controlled wildlife management. I was in the bush hunting something with every opportunity I got. Every school holiday would certainly involve hunting or fishing.

I have always been a people person and was made head boy of my high school, Falcon College, and it leaves no doubt why, when I completed my A-levels, I went directly into professional guiding. On turning 21, I started my professional hunting career. Both jobs involve and need the guides to have serious people skills if they are to be any good!

My love of bowhunting began at a young age too. I was armed with a traditional bow made from a branch of a monkey-bread tree, Piliostigma thonningii, with rawhide string, arrows from crocodile reeds, and crudely shaped broadheads from any steel I could find! I managed a dove, a francolin, a rabbit and, sorry mum... a duiker in the back yard! During my school days I yearned to start hunting with a serious bow but never had the money to buy a modern compound bow. Big guns were plenty enough fun at that time, and everyone had them. In hindsight, I am glad I went through the gun and shooting everything stage. I believe it has made me a better bowhunter, and if I never kill an animal with a gun again, that is fine with me.

3

My three years as a guide included driving a 4x4, with walking, canoeing and rafting safaris. This gave me excellent experience in approaching big game as closely and safely as possible. We had to do this and then move away from the game again without having to kill whatever we were stalking! In my home country of Zambia, one must be 21 to own a firearm, so becoming a PH happened the year I came of age.

By this time, I had had lots of big game experience, and my love of the bush was cemented - I was ready to go hunting and, more importantly, share my love of Africa with international clients. I relished the chance of sharing my knowledge and the importance of wildlife management with people from around the world. And added to that, it would be my job! Doing something I loved! WOW. How many people the world over get to wake up and say – "I love my job!"

It has been a lifelong mission of mine to get people to understand a concept that so few know about. Without hunting and proper wildlife management there will be no game left. If the local people are not taught a realistic value for their wild game, they think why keep it around? Rather destroy it all to make space for cattle, goats, chickens and donkeys which mean something to them.

The first year I was guiding alone, I had some bowhunters with me who shot compound bows heedlessly. They killed 11 animals and of those, only two were clean kills. It was horrible, and I swore never to guide another bowhunter again! By chance a year later, good friends Rassie Erasmus and Steve Kobrine hunted with me and showed me a few things. I was hooked! They showed me another side to the sport and, honestly, I would have guided my first hunt differently had I met my friends before!

I was given a 7-day crash course by Rassie and on Day 8 took a duiker and on Day 9 took a zebra and another duiker. They had created a monster! Shortly after that I ordered my first bow, a Martin Jaguar from the US. I have since bowhunted every free moment I had. I have been fortunate to have our family game ranch as a wonderful playground and schoolroom to hone my skills as a professional bowhunter. Thank you to my parents!

Living in Zambia was pretty isolating when it came to archery equipment, and pro staff for advice had been non-existent until recently. However, we now have a very nice shop in our capital, Lusaka. They can help budding archers and they are really promoting archery and 3D shoots in Zambia. All my experience, however, has been gained through books and trial and error over the last 17 years. I have also been lucky to live in a country where its residents have been able to hunt in the big game concessions surrounding our parks. Between these areas and my family ranch and various other trips to several other African nations, I have accumulated a bunch of kills, species, and wonderful experiences. Not to mention the amazing friendships made over the years! I have hunted North America and Europe extensively as well.

I have met some awesome people along my hunting trails and, though still young I have had a blessed, wonderful, and fun life. I hope to share some of my experiences and knowledge with you, the reader, hopefully to give you some pleasure and, if you are coming out here to Africa - a few good tips to make your hunting safari one of a lifetime. So many folks find that after their first trip to Africa, if it was a success, they get "The Bug": *Once Africa is in your veins, you just have to return again, and again and again.*

My book is a basic guide to bowhunting certain groups of Southern African animals, with special focus on some of the toughest species to get. It has advice on equipment, tactics, and a few stories and personal experiences. But even after reading my book, please make sure you clarify things with your outfitter. Be careful when you plan your safari over here. It is imperative you speak with your guide and know what is expected of you and what you expect of him to make your hunt a great one. This is the first important step in setting up a great hunt.

Before I continue, I would like to be very clear on something I feel strongly about. When bowhunting for any dangerous game animal - be 100% sure that your PH is a seasoned bowhunting guide. He should know when a shot is good, when a shot is bad, and when a shot is partial and will allow a second arrow. Bear in mind that you are hunting an animal that can and will kill people, especially when it is wounded. Many bowhunters will put pressure on a PH and tell him that if he shoots their animal with a gun, they will not pay for the trophy. This is bullshit! As a client, you employ a PH to do a job. Part of that job is to ensure that when a client screws up - whether it be a bad shot, bad equipment, or circumstance - he is obliged to deal with that situation so as not to endanger his group or other hunters after them. I was nearly killed once by a surprise attack from a huge buffalo bull in an area where someone had stuck an arrow in his guts and not managed to destroy him. It was swept under the carpet. But when I came past that carpet, I had to kill him at eight paces in full charge!

It is not fair or right for a client to expect a PH not to back him up, as it puts a lot of innocent people in real danger because of his screw-up. Please folks as a bowhunter, you must trust your PH and ask him to back you if the shot is bad and a second shot is unlikely - he must be the judge of this.

We are bowhunters, we are proud of this, and this is why we hunt this way because it is closer to nature, and it gives our quarry a fairer chance. Be fair to those animals and, more importantly, be fair to fellow bowhunters by not leaving a bad name in the woods.

CONTENTS

CHAPTER 1

SHOOTING FORM

Basically, to shoot long yardages, you need good form. This means your shooting technique must be solid and, with practice, should come to you like putting one foot in front of another. A bowhunter should shoot his bow often enough so that no matter what situation he finds himself in, he will react instinctively every time – kind of like driving. No matter where you stand, what the conditions are, or how excited you are, you come to the same anchor point - relax your front hand and squeeze your trigger.

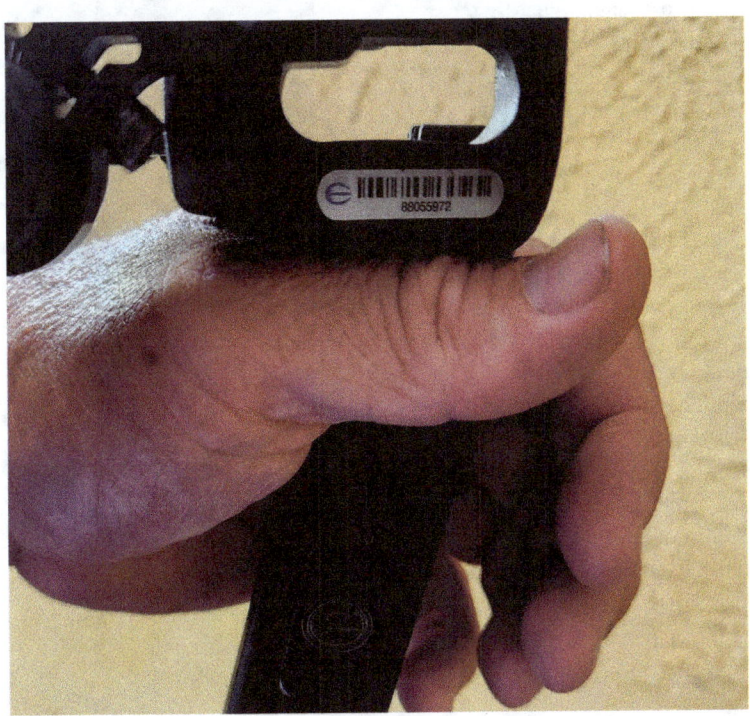

I have a little saying I always run by myself as I prepare to shoot: FPS (Feet Per Second) achieved by adhering to the following important guide: *Please see pictures to illustrate these points.*

FINGERS - Both hands relaxed, grip and trigger hand (I am a firm believer in a good mechanical release aid) The only finger to move in a shot should be the trigger one with the squeeze. Every other finger and both your hands should be totally relaxed.

PEEP - Line your peep sight up with the ring frame of your pin sight. Most sight guards today are round. This gives you another anchor point as such. Also, pick a spot. (I visualize a beating heart).

SQUEEZE - Take a breath, expel the air, hold on your spot... and gently squeeze the shot off. If you cannot hold it totally steady on your target spot, do not panic! This creates the worst "target panic" out there! Just hold as best you can and squeeze the shot off. You will be amazed how well you do.

These few points along with plenty of practice should develop good form and very tight groups

at 20 yards. Use five arrows. If you are worried about wrecking them by shooting arrows already in the target butt, move to 30 yards then 40 yards and so on. I practice at 60 yards all the time. I like to put all five arrows in a paper plate consistently from 60 to 100 yards. Always put a center spot the size of a golf ball on your paper plate to give you a spot to focus on the target.

I have converted many short-range shooters into some long-range hunters in this way. Remember you need a bow that carries the energy all the way down range. We must always be fair to the quarry we chase and use equipment that is more than capable of killing it cleanly and as quickly as possible. Today's bows in the 310fps+ range are all capable of good energy.

Shoot, enjoy it, and be confident in your ability and the performance of your bow – this is critical to achieve a long shot. If none of this works, find someone who shoots long, ask their advice and to watch you shoot, and take it from there. There are a good many archers today shooting successfully at long ranges.

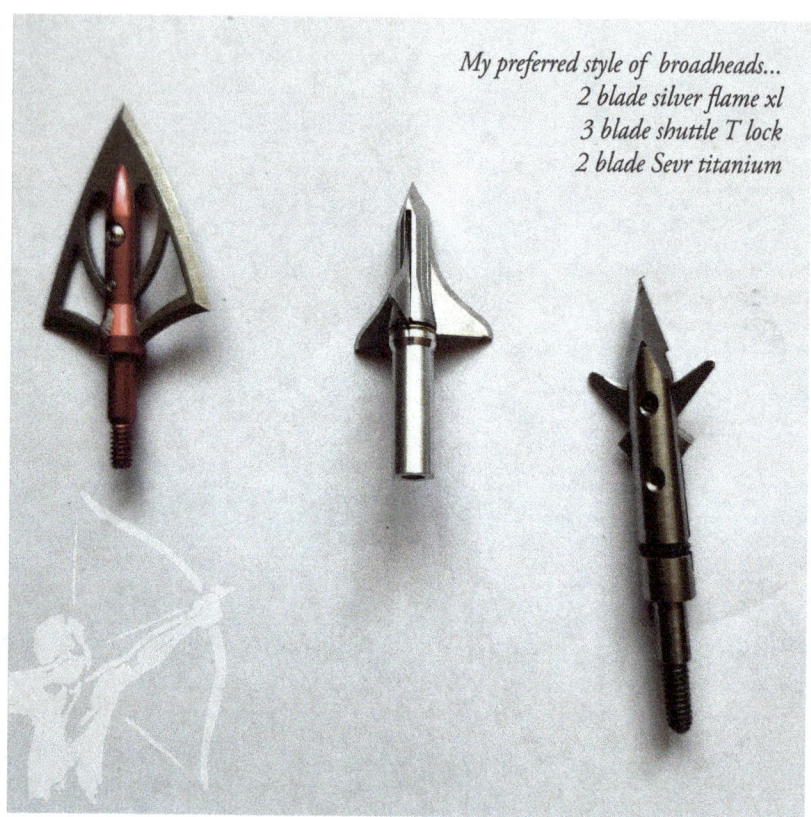

My preferred style of broadheads...
2 blade silver flame xl
3 blade shuttle T lock
2 blade Sevr titanium

Once I shot an impala ram from 112 yards. The ram lurched forward, looked around, and carried on feeding. He collapsed a few seconds later with absolutely no idea what had happened, not to mention the rest of his herd. An amazing feeling! I believe rifle hunters would compare that to something like making a 700-yard shot. Once you make a good, clean, long shot, you will be hooked and it makes your closer shots that much easier. It is also a great advantage if you ever have to follow up a wounded animal.

11

CHAPTER 2

SMALL ANTELOPE

These little guys range impressively from the tiny, royal antelope to the blue duiker, the oribi, to the Vaal rhebok. There are dozens of different species of small antelope found across Africa. From the savannas to the mountains, the coastal areas to the rain forests to the deserts, each terrain has its endemic species. These little animals are not hard to kill but are some of the toughest little critters to get a shot at. Any hunter going after Africa's little antelopes with a bow must be ready for a bunch of hard work, determination, and improvisation.

The basic equipment needed for the little guys is a bow that you can draw and hold comfortably in ANY position, whether it be sitting, kneeling, squatting, leaning, or tree standing. You want a fast carbon arrow coming out of this. Bows with a short axle-to-axle length are better for the thick bush hunts you are likely to encounter.

Choose a broadhead that works for you that will get an arrow flying its best for your rig. You must be able to "thread the needle" which means shooting through any window you are given no matter how tight! Bear in mind that often the little antelopes are in heavy cover or grass, so be sure you are happy to shoot through some stuff with your arrow. This is very possible with a good broadhead, if what you are shooting through is up close to the animal, not 10 yards or more in front! If it is too far in front, your arrow will deflect to cause a miss or, worse still, wound the animal. I love using Silver Flame 2xls made by Alaska archery. They are strong, cut big holes and fly great. Whether grass or light shrub, my arrow gets through to my target.

A good sight with pins that are bright are essential - also pins from 20 to 60 yards are important. I use a pendulum sight which is better for the longer shots but can be tough when you have a little animal that won't stay in one place. This is a personal choice.

I stick with one pin as it makes me focus better than having a mass of pins in my field of view. Like many hunters, if you find yourself tending to "flock shoot" your pins - in other words, put all the pins on the animal and let the arrow fly, change to a single pin sight, and eliminate that problem fast!

There are so many excellent bowhunting products out there so I will only cover what equipment I have found to work for me in a chapter later in the book. The archery manufacturers of the world have provided us with many wonderful gizmos and toys to last us a lifetime! We owe them a great deal for the great advances they have made in making our bowhunting adventures that much easier.

Most small antelopes live in thick cover, with scent, hearing and hiding being their top defense from predators. I hunted a Sharpe's grysbok for five years before I took one. I never hunted waterholes for them but sat at their middens where they go and poop regularly to mark territory boundaries. Hunting them like this takes lots of time - days of evening and morning hunts. Everything must be perfect with the wind being the most important.

Getting into some scent kit and being as high in a tree as possible always helps. When I got my male, I had a tree stand imprint on my backside! When he finally came in, the buck fever was out of this world and a real job to control! The grysbok is a tiny animal and shooting down from a tree was tough, but practice made perfect, and my little buck did not go far! A good broadhead placed solidly anywhere in center mass of these small animals really works.

An easier way to hunt many of these little animals is at night with a light. Make sure it is legal where you do it and practice shooting at a target with a light - it is different! Aligning your peep is hard but vital at night. Sights with a glow-in-the-dark frame are a good idea. Always be sure to use a range finder too. Things always seem a lot further at night.

Alternative means of hunting are walk and stalk, blinds or stands at waterholes, and calling, which is amazing to experience if you have a caller that knows his stuff.

Your PH should know what works best in the area he is guiding you.

I once hunted thick riverine, coastal forest for blue duiker with a friend. We had a tracker with us who would set up, much like when elk hunting, and call these duikers in. So often the duikers would come in so fast that we only had a fleeting glance. Shots were really tough, and we ended up taking all the pins off his sight except one - set at 20 yards. When the duikers would come flitting through, he would judge, compensate, and let fly! Many vines, branches, logs and twigs were broken before he finally made contact with his little blue duiker. Those trackers who call have an amazing talent to bring in small antelope.

In contrast, species like oribi, steenbok and Vaal rhebok live mainly in vast open areas with sight and speed being their number one defense mechanisms. I know of very few hunters who have taken Vaal rhebok, found in South Africa, with a bow. Rhebok typically live in open, often hilly to mountainous areas. The few I am aware of have been shot on driven hunts and from using a pop-up blind and a decoy.

When I helped on one particular hunt, many of the mountains had flat tops where the rhebok lived. By positioning hunters on well-used routes on the top of a mountain and driving the length of the plateau with beaters, it offered shots to a few guys. Very often, the rhebok would stop as it was about to descend from the top. If a hunter was smart, ready, and aware, he would get his ram like this.

I sat with one guy and we set up behind a big rock. We heard the rhebok coming our way and prepared ourselves. I was filming. The females came past at a trot about 20 yards from us and, as we watched, the ram came flying over our rock and headed to a screeching halt 40 yards from us, and my hunter let fly! I think the excitement was too much - the arrow sailed over the animal's back by about two feet! This was about our fifth drive, so a tough one to swallow. Sadly, he never got his rhebok.

Another hunter got a stuffed decoy and set it up in a ram's territory. He set up a pop-up blind about 50 yards away and would get in there before sun-up and spend the day there. Sure enough, after a few days, the group of rhebok showed up and the dominant ram came straight in to check out the decoy. The hunter got his rhebok. Great plan, but access to decoys is very limited!

Oribi are always a great challenge and highly sought after. These little animals really like wide open spaces and are difficult to get. The best way to hunt them is by spot and stalk in the late evening and early mornings. Oribi love burnt areas, so start here if there are any around. I know one place where I hunt that sets up their oribi hunters well. Every year, they will control-burn strips of grass about 150 yards wide through areas of high grass. When the new, green shoots of the grass come through, the oribi go to these like bees to nectar. To hunt them, we simply cruise the edge of the burns until a good oribi is spotted in the distance. You can then set yourself up with the wind and use all the high unburnt grass to stalk your ram. Often shots are in the 40-yard range but prepare yourself to shoot out to 70 yards for the little guys, and really prepare for string jumping - they are fast! Not always, but when they do jump, you normally miss them.

The common duiker is probably the one little antelope that is seen most in Southern Africa. Because they are small, don't underestimate little guys. I know of one hunter who shot a common duiker far back and high. The duiker collapsed and the hunter went to cut the little animal's throat to finish him off. Before he knew it, the ram had swung round and sunk both his horns four inches into the man's thigh! Had the duiker's aim been higher and had he got the man's femoral artery, it could have been a much worse story. There are several known cases of domesticated duiker having killed people by piercing the femoral.

Every Southern African country has its "own" specific tiny animals. They all offer fun hunting and a challenge for any hunter.

CHAPTER 3

SWAMP ANTELOPE

There are specific antelopes that live in swampy areas, namely the lechwes and the sitatunga. For these you want a bow with a minimum of 70lbs to carry enough energy out to 70 yards and you must be proficient with this distance. There are times when you can get closer shots, but not often because of the normally open habitat. Again, a good arrow with a solid broadhead is a must to hunt these animals.

When hunting lechwes, the best way to get close, for me, has been to set up in a clump of reeds, close to main trails. Lechwe will normally move out of the wet areas in the mornings to dry ground. They dry for the day and then move towards the swamp to feed again in the evening. Set up on a well-worn game trail between them and with the right wind, and hope for a shot at a male before they see or smell you. When hunting the Kafue for black lechwe, you could have a couple thousand animals coming past you. I do not think there are many places left on earth where you find this sort of natural numbers of animals. It is truly an amazing spectacle and something very special to see.

Pick your animal and focus on him. Make sure he is clear in case of a pass-through, and then pick a spot. You must focus on this very carefully as it can be disconcerting with so many animals around.

While the typical perfectly shaped lechwe horns always look nice, watch for the odd-shaped ones. These will often hold the greatest length.

I once set up on a trail for a group of Kafue lechwe (endemic to Zambia's Kafue Flats). There were only about 26 of them out in a million acres of grass short as a carpet. I chose what I thought was the best route between them and the wetlands and waited. I chose to hunt this group as one of the males had very tightly shaped horns that looked weird and came in very close at the tips. This one intrigued me. Shape did not matter. What were the chances those few lechwes would come past me? After two hours of sitting in the sun with clusters of very irritating lechwe flies on me (they don't bite, but crawl on and into you the whole time), the herd started coming my way. As it turned out they did not use our trail but another, which would put the animal I wanted at 73 yards when I shot. As he walked, I knew I

could not shoot at him walking - not at that range. So I bleated like a fawn; he stopped, and my arrow flew. It went in behind the shoulder and lodged in the opposite one. He ran 25 yards and piled up. When I got to him, I was astounded. Although he had funny horns, I could see he was a good specimen. I am awaiting official measurements, but he may be the biggest lechwe taken of all time, rifle, or bow. I shot this lechwe in a place that loads of hunters pass every week in the season. I guess because he looked weird, he had been overlooked and never blasted with a .300 - or maybe I just got lucky. But he made me proud and has a prime spot on my wall!

You also get the red lechwe in Zambia, South Africa, Namibia, and Botswana. Then another one endemic to Zambia alone is the black lechwe of the Bangweulu Wetlands. You would hunt these in pretty much the same way as the Kafue lechwe.

The black lechwe numbers are doing really well and make for some amazing experiences. I set up in a clump of weeds a couple years ago and sat for about three hours till I saw a cloud of dust coming my way. What emerged from the dust was a herd of lechwe rams that I believe numbered about 2000 animals! They came past and around me and smelt me, so started running. For about 30 minutes I could hardly see let alone breathe for dust from all the animals. I never even got a shot! It is truly one of the most epic moments in my bowhunting career.

Another swamp animal is one of Africa's ultimate and most coveted antelope - the Zambezi sitatunga. Few bowhunters have taken these animals. I know many have done the forest sitatunga which inhabits the rainforests to the North, but the Zambezi is a tough customer.

Hunting them involves finding a clearing in the thick swamps where you have lots of crocodile reeds and papyrus, which is important, as sitatunga feed and live in this. If you can find a clearing which has been burnt and has fresh shoots... that is first prize. Scout as best as you can to find a clearing that the sitatunga use a lot and have left plenty of tracks and feeding sign. On the downwind side of this you either need to build a blind or a machan (elevated stand), bearing in mind there are no trees.

The machan is the normal thing to do as often there is too much weed to get a good clear shot from a blind. It is then purely a waiting game with the hope that if a male comes out, he is within bow range of you. This is where long-range shooting is invaluable. It is imperative to make a good shot as a wounded sitatunga will dive into the deepest, thickest nastiest cover, water, or swamp, and be almost impossible to recover. When alarmed or wounded a sitatunga is known to go out into deep water and submerge its whole body with only nostrils sticking out to breathe. That makes for some hard trailing.

Be prepared to get very wet, be sucked by leeches, bitten by mosquitoes, and itch from the reeds, and be on constant alert for crocs. If you go there between May and August be sure to take waders and warm clothes - it gets bitterly cold, and being wet in this sucks! Often it will be necessary to wade out to your machan if you want to be in good sitatunga territory.

This is a very tough hunt and is normally seven days of grueling hunting, and the success rate really is 50/50. Be sure to speak to your outfitter carefully about this hunt and be prepared for possible failure. It is not easy.

In my opinion Zambia is the place for all the southern swamp species, with the Kafue and black lechwe only occurring there. They also have good numbers of red lechwe in the North Kafue.

The Bangweulu Swamp is home to the sitatunga and a few private enterprises like Wildlive's Game Ranch, and Shiwa N'gandu and Kafue Fisheries that have them on their properties. These private ranches are a good and more certain hunt for the bowhunter.

21

CHAPTER 4

MEDIUM-SIZED ANTELOPE

Medium-sized plains game is the impala, reedbuck, bushbuck, puku, springbok and blesbok. These animals are probably the most shot antelopes in Southern Africa. This is purely because they are so common. I know some would say puku are not as they are endemic to Zambia. However, in Zambia there are loads of them.

A bow of 60lbs and up with a good carbon arrow, tipped with a good broadhead is the ticket. In the case of these animals, hunters can try out

their broadheads with larger cutting diameters as these animals are not as hard as the big ones. Don't get me wrong here - a badly placed shot on these animals, and you have a very tough trailing session ahead of you.

The impala is probably the most common and well-known medium-sized animal in Southern Africa. You get the southern, eastern, and black-faced impala - along with a few black

and white ones in South Africa. Anyone coming on a hunting safari in Southern Africa will for sure encounter the impala during their travels. It is a worthy adversary and I guess equates to the whitetail in the USA. They are plentiful right across the continent and generally have a pretty cheap price tag on them.

They are smart, alert, fast, string-jumpy, a species I have shot hundreds of, but I never tire of hunting a good one. They can be hunted in many ways – at waterholes, from tree stands, walk and stalk, spot and stalk - you name it.

When shooting one of these animals, be sure to aim as low as possible on their vitals. Nine out of ten times they will jump the string. I saw a picture my friend took of an impala that was almost lying on the ground. Behind it there was a cloud of dust where an arrow was striking the ground. The shot was taken from 18 yards. Fast!

I once set up on a trail with a group of impalas feeding towards me. The lead animal came up the trail and stopped at 19 yards, head up and staring. I was at full draw by this stage and decided that my 80lb bow would send the arrow down his throat and out the rear end. I settled in to the shot and let her fly. The impala ran about 80yards and piled up. On inspection, my arrow was sticking out the front shoulder. Odd. In that 19-yard flight my arrow made, the impala had managed to do a 180 degree turn and the arrow entered through its rump and traversed the body. Very fast.

When impala rams go into the rut in April/May it is an amazing time to hunt them. They beef up their necks, get very vocal, running around roaring, something like a lion. The rams go into this frenzy between two moon phases. Like with whitetails, it is now you see the really big ones out and about. The rams run hard looking for females, and herd rams have about 20 odd days to breed with his ewes as well as fight off other hungry studs. If a ram has 100 ewes... you do the math. By the end of it, the herd ram is totally pooped!

One of the reasons impala do so well is that while the ram is chasing off one intruder, another will slip in and spread his oats quickly. This makes for an amazing genetic base in a herd. The rams' rutting brings the ewes into season for breeding. This time is awesome for hunting impala - survival tends to slip on their priority list.

Funnily enough, the impala in Southern Zambia also seems to be a mini version of its southern counterparts. It is the same species but much smaller in body and horn shape. A 22-inch impala in South Africa is an average male. To Zambians, this is almost unheard of - Mother Nature making all

shapes and sizes to fit every ecosystem.

South Africa is often a hunter's first safari destination. Springbok and blesbok are super common animals here and will be encountered often on a safari. They are open plains animals and longer shots are the norm to get them, so ensure you are confident out to 60 yards at least. Blesbok may be taken at water but springbok do not need to drink often, so stalking is often the way to hunt them. Stalking a blesbok on foot can be a real challenge and provides for some good hunting – expect long shots.

There are several types of springbok - common, black, white, and copper. They are symbolic of the desert areas and South Africa. A must species when you are there. The bushbuck deserves special mention. This medium-sized animal is truly beautiful. There are many subspecies including Cape, Limpopo, Chobe, and harnessed bushbucks. It is part of the spiral horn family and has spots and stripes and stunning markings. They are secretive creatures and need to be hunted either at water, over a food source such as at a sausage or fig tree, or by walk and stalk.

Morning and evening are the best times to hunt them, with big rams often shot at water during midday.

A friend stalked and shot a Chobe bushbuck feeding in an alfalfa field early one morning. The arrow hit him a bit far back. He decided to put his dog on the animal as he had almost no blood to follow in the heavy

cover surrounding the field. It did not take long for the dog to bay the animal. As my buddy approached the wounded bushbuck, the ram took one look at him, forgot the dog and charged. The bushbuck lodged a horn between his thighs up against the jewels and the other alongside the outside of his thigh. It proceeded to drive him around the bush like that for a while until he managed to

24

grab an overhanging branch and lift himself away from the enraged animal. At that point the bushbuck took off again with the dog in hot pursuit and my buddy managed to finish it off with a rifle. The grazes on either side of his thigh were testimony to the fact that inches could have cost his life. The bushbuck is fierce and dangerous when it is wounded or cornered. Treat them with extreme respect. There are many cases of people being killed by an enraged bushbuck.

Bushbuck as I mentioned love riverine and thick bush. If you can find a fig tree or sausage tree in these areas or even a jacaranda tree close to an urban area, these are great places to put your stand and wait for a hungry old male. I suggested this to another friend who is an avid bowhunter. On his second day on a stand in a large fig tree, he had a good ram come in. Being

his first close encounter with a good bushbuck male, he began to draw his bow, heart pounding and arms trembling. His tree stand was purely a branch of the old fig tree. During the excitement and exertion of the draw process, he slipped and slid round the branch. In his defense, fig tree bark is pretty smooth. But how on earth he hung there, upside down and still attempted the shot is a mystery to me and

no doubt goes down in the bushbuck's life story as a hilarious and lucky day.

The common reedbuck is a secretive animal, living in grasslands with tall grass as cover. Spot and stalk is the order here, and the higher you can be on a truck or horse, the better. This allows you a great vantage point to spot and mark a reedbuck male. Do this late evening and early mornings when they are most active. Be sure to use a well-constructed broadhead as you are more than likely going to be shooting through some grass. They are never far from water either, but most often they feed and drink at night.

Puku is a Zambian species that many archers come to Zambia for. They are a good-looking animal and commonly found throughout the country. They frequent areas close to water like floodplains and grassy valleys. Catch them late in the evening or early in the morning when they will have their heads down, filling their guts. This makes them a really fun animal to stalk with a bow.

CHAPTER 5

LARGE ANIMALS

Animals in the large plains-game section are hartebeest, waterbuck, oryx, kudu, eland, sable, roan, zebra, and wildebeest, and there are several sub-species of the above. if you are prepared to take any of these animals your equipment will handle most plains game around.

Your bow should be a minimum of 60lb draw weight. A solid carbon arrow tipped with a good broadhead is essential. My personal choice are Grizzly Stiks from Alaska Archery - their TDT arrows are amazing. The Grizzly Stiks are made with a natural forward of center which helps arrow flight and penetration immensely. I like my arrows to be between 500 and 550gr TAW, and I am happy if they are tipped with Sevr or Shuttle T-LOK broadheads. If you get your pro shop to set up all your kit, ask them to set your arrows up so they are capable of killing a moose - then you are ready for our larger plains-game species.

African plains game has an amazing tenacity for staying alive - it just seems to be wired into them - they are tough. I guess we would be too if we had evolved with every bush, nook, cranny and creek having some sort of critter in it that could potentially kill or eat us! Unlike North American game, the vitals on our plains game sit far forward - when shooting any of them, aim as far forward as possible, right up behind the shoulder.

Both the red hartebeest and Lichtenstein's hartebeest are taken either at water, salt licks or stalking. These are two of the fastest antelopes we have, so are generally well wired! Be sure to aim in the bottom third of the vital area because nine times out of ten they will jump the string. I have lost many a hartebeest with high shoulder shots. Once this happens, they take off roaring at high speed and disappear into the horizon leaving no blood trail to follow at all. This gut-wrenching feeling really sucks, and unless your PH has a top, super-fit tracking dog, your trophy is lost.

The waterbuck is a great trophy to have. There are several types, but the two main ones are the common waterbuck found right across Southern Africa and the Defassa waterbuck which has a dark face and completely white butt. Unique only to Zambia is the Crawshay's Defassa waterbuck, and with a small, un-huntable pocket in Angola. They are smaller than the common and have a completely white backside as opposed to the ring

on the common's butt. Though the horns are smaller, they are stunning-looking animals. Waterbuck are always associated with water as their name aptly suggests. They are best hunted at water or, of course, by stalking them.

I sat at a waterhole one day for a common waterbuck bull that had been seen often in that area. He was supposedly a good bull and the cover around there was very thick thorn scrub. I like to spot and stalk, or walk and stalk, but this particular bull had to be hunted at water. I got into my ground blind around 3.30 in the afternoon. The bull arrived at very last light. He stood a mere 12 yards from me. Slam dunk? Well, I let my arrow fly at the then quartering away bull who was busy drinking. He jumped my string so badly that the last time I saw him my arrow stuck out high on his back almost straight up! The ranch owner did not have a dog and I never found my bull. The arrow was high enough and far enough back that he would be able to lick and clean the wound. Knowing this, I believe he would have survived that shot with no problem. Over the years, I have learnt that if an animal can reach a high body shot to clean it, he will survive. If the animal cannot reach the wound, like if it's in his upper neck - infection will set in and generally the animal will succumb to the shot after a long, agonizing time.

Hunting the Defassa is the same as for the common, and most people do not like waterbuck meat. The animal has glands in its skin which secret an oily film to protect it from water and bugs. This stuff really stinks and makes them very strong smelling. However, I have learnt that if you take a waterbuck and begin skinning and gutting him immediately, the meat is actually pretty damn good. It is imperative that you do not touch the meat with the same hand that is holding the skin. Once that oil contacts the meat - the stink is in! We are blessed that all our game makes excellent table fare. So much is in the preparation, like with any meal.

The oryx is a desert animal and is common to South Africa, Botswana, and Namibia. It is a big animal with great long horns and a lust for life second to none. They are incredibly tough and require a very well-placed shot for a good clean kill. They are mostly hunted at water and by stalking. They are aggressive, which is a good thing because if a hunter makes a bad shot, and the PH has a dog, an oryx stops up pretty quick for a fight.

It is very important to shoot an oryx as far forward as possible. Right up against the shoulder, because the guts on an oryx push a long way forward. I learned this when I made a shot on my first bull that would kill most game real quick. My PH's dog was fully engaged, but a couple hours later, I had to shoot a second time.

The kudu. Anyone who knows this animal or has an interest in hunting in Africa, will most likely know that this antelope is always high on every trophy hunter's list. It also ranks highly with the meat hunter. There are many ways to hunt a kudu bull and all of them lead to a final sequence of events which is amazing to even the seasoned bowhunter. When that kudu bull first steps out into plain view, it is so awe inspiring that if you do not get excited, there is something wrong with you! Kudu are hunted over feed, at water and, in May or June, hunting them in the rut on foot is awesome.

The bulls are everywhere then, and very much have one thing on the brain!

I was driving along a river line on a free-range cattle ranch in Namibia with a buddy of mine. It was May and the bulls had begun their wanderings. We were actually driving the area, looking for the tracks of a big male leopard that was killing cattle. As we went past an opening which gave us a good view of a length of dry riverbed, I spotted a kudu about 400 yards away. We stopped, backed up and glassed the bull. He was a monster. The owner of the ranch told me, "If you can kill him with your bow, on foot - he is yours." Wow! My kind of man. They dropped me and carried on looking for tracks, and I donned my leafy suit and begun my stalk. I slowly made my way along a game trail that wound along the edge of the river. It was great to have this as it silenced my footsteps. This is always a tough proposition in Africa. I like to hunt in any shoe with a crepe sole or, if possible, in a thick pair of socks or bare foot. These seem to be the quietest ways of getting into game.

By the time I reached the spot which I had marked in my mind, the kudu bull had gone. I went into stealth mode and inched my way forward, painstakingly slowly. The slower you can move when stalking here, the better. During one of my pauses, I heard thrashing of limbs up ahead – but no elephant here. I moved in slowly, and there on the edge of the river was the kudu. He had his head buried in a big bush with his backside sticking out. The beautiful corkscrew horns poked their way out of the top of the bush. This bull was marking his area and showing off his dominance to anyone interested. As he thrashed the branches, I moved closer. I reached the edge of the river and had a clear line of sight 44 yards to the bull across the sandy river bottom. I nocked my arrow and poised myself for the draw, but he was too deep into the bush and his vitals were obscured.

After what seemed an eternity, the kudu took two small steps back and exposed his chest. The arrow entered slightly back and left of his front shoulder. He lurched high into the air, piled back into the bush and disappeared out the other side. I went up and found his death run only lasted some 45 yards. To date he is the biggest bull I have shot with a bow, measuring a whopping 58 inches with massive bases. Had he not been rutting like a mad thing, I doubt I would have taken that beautiful animal that way.

The eland is Africa's biggest antelope and part of the spiral horn family. These animals grow huge, and with a big bull weighing up to 2000lbs, he is quite a slab of meat to hunt. Hunters really need to be sure their equipment can handle a moose! And that meat is also one of the best there is in our antelopes. Eland are hunted at water in the drier months and over feed. Spot and walk and stalk are also very effective, although the eland's size and height gives him an elevated view which is hard to get under.

As bulls reach maturity, around six or seven years of age, they become a dark blue color during breeding season. As they get older (eight plus) they stay like that and they are often referred to as "blue bulls". They truly are impressive animals at this stage, with big swinging dewlaps and an audible click that resounds from their knees as they move along. No one really knows the purpose of the clicking noise they produce, but it will often alert a hunter on stand to an approaching eland.

The majestic sable is classed by many as the pinnacle of magnificence when it comes to antelopes. He is a little more expensive to hunt and is a species that returning hunters to Africa will often set their goals on. The pitch-black bulls with white face markings and long curving horns toward the back are impressive to say the least. Bulls may also be brown in color. Be careful when shooting these, as sable cows are also brown. Most often, sable will be hunted by spot and stalk. They can be taken at water too, but are not reliable on their drinking patterns. I would suggest a PH is a good idea to have with you when you shoot your prize sable bull to ensure you shoot a decent trophy - they are very tough to judge as even the smaller bulls look good!

A wounded sable is easily stopped by a good dog as he will not take nonsense from anyone and will readily turn to fight his tormentor.

A family friend once wounded a bull by hitting him too far back. A common rule for us in bowhunting here is that if you make a shot too far back - leave the animal at least three hours before following up. By doing this, your animal will normally try to lie up quickly if undisturbed. This gives him a chance to either die or get sick, which will offer you a  second shot. It sounds cruel but is far better than going after him too soon and flushing him out of his first chosen spot. This would get him on the move and kick in the lifesaving adrenalin rush. Most times, should this happen, recovery of your trophy is rare and it leads to a much longer and crueler death. Take your time.

After about three and a half hours, our friend went after his bull. The tracks were good and there was some blood so following was relatively easy. After some 600 yards, he spotted his bull lying next to a large rock in the photo position with its head curled back against its body. Our friend came round the rock and prodded the bull in its neck from behind. Before he knew it, the sweeping horns came flying back and buried right through his intestines. It was a long recovery and an extensive doctor's bill.

31

ROAN

This antelope is bigger in body than the sable but has smaller horns. It is recognized as an endangered species and thus is hard to come by and, when you do - has a pretty price tag attached to it. They can be very tough to hunt but are patternable at water and salt licks, particularly later in the year. Again, like the sable, pay attention to this animal as he is not afraid to get down and dirty and put up a good fight.

ZEBRA

The zebra is also a species which is iconic of Africa and most hunters should and will hunt one. For all those horse lovers out there - the zebra is generally un-tamable as many folks out here have found out. They are mean critters that bite and kick at every chance. Zebra rugs and mounts are truly beautiful and will look great in your house.

A buddy of mine told me a story about a so-called tame zebra. He was hunting on a ranch for oryx with some clients. As he approached a gate in a cattle paddock the local "tame" zebra stallion approached the truck on the passenger side. The client was on top of the truck and his wife sat in the passenger seat with their small son in the middle. The zebra came right up to the window. Cute, hey?
He proceeded to push his head through the window across the laps of wife and child and begun the process of destroying the steering wheel. It was a messy affair for the cab but a good thing my buddy carried a side arm! It was later learnt that the same zebra had attacked and killed a trespasser on the said ranch. Tore chunks out of his legs

and kicked the you-know-what out of him - and they still had the animal around! All wild animals - even if raised in the best homes - will always maintain a wild streak in them somewhere. These streaks often have fatal consequences to humans.

Zebra are very common and can be found all over Southern Africa with various sub-species occurring. These animals are super sharp and wide awake. All the zebra's senses are acutely keen. No matter where I have hunted across Africa, they always seem to be wild as the wind. The zebra is best hunted at water or on foot and provides a real challenge to the bowhunter. It is said that to ensure a clean kill, a hunter must shoot the zebra right behind the shoulder and on a black stripe - a hit on the white stripe and you will have a wounded animal! And like all our game, the zebra is no exception - he will go forever with a mediocre shot.

WILDEBEEST

The wildebeest is often referred to as, "the poor man's buffalo". Again, common to Southern Africa it is an obvious choice for any bowhunter on an African safari. String-jumpy, tenacious and wary, the wildebeest has well earned his reputation for being as tough as a buffalo and is somewhat similar in appearance. The great wildebeest migrations in Zambia and Tanzania/Kenya are some of the largest in the world and are a true spectacle.

The wildebeest can be hunted at water, salt licks, feed blocks or by stalking. Bulls will cover their territories morning and evening, making a bellowing sound. This is useful to pinpoint them when out on a walk. One year I hunted a particular bull on a friend's ranch in South Africa. He was an old bull with worn-down horns and not much left to him in terms of trophy quality, but he had a massive body - great meat value. My friend described where he had been seeing this bull and I spent a couple days walking there to familiarize myself with the animal's trails and middens. The area was very thick, crisscrossed with a few roads, and these were intersected with game trails.

A few days later while I was walking in the evening, I heard bellows. I moved in closer to try to get an idea of where and what the bull was doing - if it was even the said bull. As I closed the gap, it became apparent that he was working along a well-worn game trail which, from my scouting, had several middens along it. The trail led across and with the prevailing wind which was perfect. So with a rapid scuffle I looped around and ahead of the bull to a spot where I felt would be good to set up. After a wait of about 35 minutes, the old bull came bumbling down the trail. I had set up in a bush just off the trail on the edge of a clearing. There was a midden there about 30 yards away and I felt he would stop and mill around there for a bit, offering a shot. For some reason, today he was not stopping at that midden and came on straight toward me. I decided to draw my bow anyway and see what would happen. As my string came back, the bull obviously saw something and came to a halt about 12 yards away. His head went high and he stood tall. At that moment, he looked bigger than a Cape buffalo!! I sent the arrow into his chest right at the base of his throat. There was a loud sucking sound and the bull lurched high in the air and bounded not away, but straight into my bush of concealment – no worries, I was making a nifty escape by this stage! He ran about 70 yards and fell stoners. The bull had been in his death run and I don't believe he was after me at all.

If you ever hunt a wildebeest at water or a salt lick be sure to aim low - in the bottom third, not half way up. They are very jumpy and will react to a shot 99% of the time. Obviously be sure to aim at the very bottom of the vitals in case you do by some chance get an animal with lead in its feet!

CHAPTER 6

SWINE

This covers the pigs - one of my favorite and challenging hunts, and of many bow hunters I know. The main pig in Southern Africa is warthog and bushpig. The Congo and Cameroon offer the red river hog and giant forest hog. There are some places in South Africa that have the European boar now as well.

Our pigs are incredibly tough and tenacious animals, particularly the bushpig. When hunting them, I like to have a bow of 50-60lbs or higher if possible. They are solid animals, so I recommend as heavy a carbon arrow as possible for your setup, armed with a well-constructed broadhead. In other words, don't use an expandable with a 2½ inch cutting diameter – rather go with a 1¼ inch.

I don't mind expandable broadheads but there is a rule I have when clients are using them.

I feel that more bow hunters would use and respect expandables if everyone stuck to this basic rule:

Bows with poundage up to 55lbs should use expandables with a cutting diameter no bigger than 1 1/8 inches.

55-65lb bows should go no bigger than 1¼ inches.

65-75lb bows should go no bigger than 1 inch.

75-80lb bows can launch expandables over 1½ inches

By using these guidelines, you will have better blade deployment, better penetration, and great arrow flight to boot.

When choosing my arrows for pigs and large plains game, I like to look at the yardage my type of arrows can achieve and shoot as heavy an arrow as possible without going into big game status with inserts, etc. I will cover this better in another chapter.

What every bowhunter must remember is that expandable broadheads need lots of energy to be deployed - make sure your equipment has what it takes. The beauty of an expandable is that they are so easy to tune and get flying. If you have the energy, they are lethal, and with heavier poundages you can get very large wound channels. I really like the Sevr Titanium range of expandables.

I shoot Alaska Archery Silver Flame XXL broadheads for everything and they are deadly, dependable, and great penetrating machines. Fixed blade heads are a solid choice and if this works for you and you can get them flying well and like your field points – great. The smaller diameter fixed blades of today are tough and offer great penetration. If I shoot a 3 Blade Head, it will be a trophy ridge Shuttle T-Lok… they fly great, are strong, and cut big holes.

We are fortunate today to have such an amazing variety of equipment available with great options of choice – use them wisely and explore your options and you will reap great rewards. Speak to hunters that have had experience with whatever choice you are making. Most bow hunters are happy to share advice. Just be sure to have a tried and tested rig that shoots straight, and you are confident with.

Warthogs are generally hunted at waterholes and this method is very effective. Walk and stalk can be awesome fun too. Warthog and bushpig have relatively poor eyesight but their other senses are excellent, so pay attention to wind and sound. I have found some of my biggest pigs in mountains. If you are hunting for warthog in an area that has hills, take a walk up there. For some reason, those big old boars love to go and hide away up high. Warthogs love rooting for rhizomes, a bulbous root at the base of several species of our tall grasses growing higher than the hip, and if you can find an area that has  been burnt, even better. The lack of surface cover makes the pig's job easier to root. If you find an area that has been dug up by pigs - come back to it morning and evening. Pigs will return regularly to a favorite feeding spot. If you spot a big one leaving a feeding area, keep working it - he will be back.

I once took a warthog on a cattle ranch. The pigs were totally free range here, but I was driving past a feeding area for the cattle which consisted of a bare trampled area dotted with old truck tires filled with feed and molasses (sugar cane derivative). As I went past, one tire had a large butt sticking out of it. Evidently, with his head buried in the sweets, the warthog had not heard me coming. When he lifted his head, I saw he was a beauty, but he took off at full speed. There was a large tree 40 yards away and at a good angle to the tires he had been feeding at. I piled two tires next to the trees and returned early the next morning to sit behind them. My shooting lane was between the tree and tires. I waited and waited and begun wondering if I had scared him off. I had been there three hours when I saw him coming at a trot, straight to his tire from yesterday. He came head on and buried himself, butt in the air, in the feed. I waited for what seemed an eternity for him to eventually shovel himself around the rim of the tire into a shooting position. The big old boar never knew where it came from or what hit him. He did not even make it out of the feeding area.

Warthogs tend to scrape the ground away with their noses making

shallow scrapes. Bushpig tend more to gouge the ground. So, if you are looking for specific pig activity, bear this in mind. The bushpig loves digging big holes and making long rooting lines with his nose. The warthog seems more clinical and tidier.

Old warthogs, like all animals, are smart... you must outthink them. On private properties where hunting pressure can be hard and there is minimal predator activity, old boars will be active at last light and into the night. I shot one of my biggest warthogs at 7.45 p.m. while in a tree stand by water with bait there for bushpig. But he was not interested in me or my bait - just the water. I, however, was very interested in him!

When booking a hunt, if warthog is high on the list - ask your PH when the rut is. It is normally around April/May. If you get there during the warthog rut, it is amazing. There will be big, good quality pigs everywhere. They are much like kudu or whitetail during the rut - they get dumb and throw caution to the wind. The two pigs shown were both in the rut. I shot mine on foot as he chased a sow, while my wife sat at a waterhole watching two sows when her big old boar came sniffing. The crossbow bolt rendered him lifeless in 30 yards.

Bushpigs... that is another creature! They are ALL smart, all tough, almost impossible to pattern, and one of my favorite species to hunt. I have taken many animals that I do not wish to shoot again, but bushpigs I never tire of.

One of my best ways to hunt them is over bait. I like to sour corn/maize in a drum of water with a couple pounds of sugar. I normally leave this concoction for about three weeks before I use it. I like to scout for pig activity and then set up my bait downwind of where I feel the pigs will bed down. They are strictly nocturnal so the closer to a bedding area (without disturbing them) the better. I have found over time that a tree stand is far better than sitting on the ground. I honestly feel that a bushpig picks up vibration in the ground, and when he is approaching a bait on full alert, he uses this sense a lot. We all shuffle our feet at some point. I have had many cases where I just cannot work out why the pigs never came. Wind perfect, sitting still, but... I have much more success with pigs out of a tree stand. I normally let them eat three nights in a row and then sit. This has given me the best success, with them

arriving early and still in daylight shooting hours. The bait is still new in their minds, tastes good and they cannot get enough of it.

Once they have been feeding for a while, their feed times tend to become erratic, and sitting in a tree stand into the early hours of the morning is not my idea of humor.

The earliest I have shot a bushpig at a bait is 4.30 in the afternoon, and several others as dark is settling in. Many are taken just after dark.

I love to walk and stalk for bushpig. Concentrate along riverbeds, the edge of valleys. If you know where they bed and it is an accessible area - this can be a very effective stalk, too. When the first rains arrive - get out there late in the evening in known pig country, look for spoor and track them. This is an incredibly rewarding, thrilling, and the ultimate way of hunting.

The biggest pig I ever took was a boar I hunted for four years. I baited him, I tracked him, I tried to catch him bedding... impossible. He had a very large track and his right front hoof twisted to the right which made him unique and identifiable. One December afternoon we had a good rainstorm, and once it cleared, I grabbed my bow and headed for the monster's territory. I had been crisscrossing an area for about an hour when I crossed a sounder's tracks. They were feeding, and his track was among them. I began to follow and, like so, so many times before, this old boar led them feeding down wind. I decided to follow anyway. I had not been with the tracks long when, with the residual storm clouds, the wind changed and started to blow into my face - a chance perhaps? I must have cut their track freshly behind them as it was soon after the lucky change that I spotted the first pig. I was

standing next to a bush in my leafy suit, now watching three or four of them feeding when he entered the arena from some thick grass to my left. As he came through, the others very quickly gave him full right of way. As he scuffled with a younger pig, I drew my bow and held. That day I was using my 80lb Mathews Black Max which made those 30-odd seconds brutal. He turned and started feeding, quartering away at about 43 yards. My 600-grain arrow entered his right hip and exited the opposite shoulder. He took off roaring, made a huge circle and came right back my way! I held my bow baseball bat style and prepared to strike, run, dive - none of which I was 100% would work! The boar passed me at five yards - still not seeing me. He ran into a tree the thickness of a man's leg, recovered, stood up on his back legs and fell over dead. He had been running dead, but it scared the hell out of me. Silence followed. The only thing I could hear was my own heart. As the sounds of the bush started coming back to me, I sat down by that monster. My nemesis. It was one of my best, most thrilling and, to this day, proudest hunts ever. I took about an hour to load the beast onto my truck. Many ropes, sticks, fulcrums and plans later, I managed to load the pig which later turned out to hit the scales at 246lbs. Truly a great pig when an average boar weighs about 120lbs.

That pig and hundreds more have probably given me the most hunting pleasure ever. And the closest I have come so far to being eaten by an animal has been by a bushpig. I was out taking a walk and carrying my .375 rifle as a back-up weapon when I came across where a large sable bull had been killed fighting with another. As I was kicking around some bones I heard a terrific roaring and screaming that is only made by a bushpig. I turned, and hurtling towards me from my right, came this boar. I unslung the rifle, threw it up, sliding the safety off and simultaneously fired. Again, silence. The pig lay at my feet with a large hole in the top of his head, its contents sprayed all over my legs and feet. It was close. That charge was for no reason, and to this day I do not have any idea why he came after me, apart from the supposition that he was upset at me intruding on his bone and calcium supply.

Often, when guys hunt bushpigs in their corn fields out here, the hunter will make the pig aware of his presence and then just wait for the pig to come to him! Bear in mind this can happen at night in some pretty thick stuff. The pigs are often very vocal and sound huge and seem everywhere! It is very exciting. Pigs are scavengers and will eat almost anything, so piles of offal and old carcasses are great places to find them.

Please be aware that a wounded or cornered bushpig is extremely dangerous and will attack. Several dogs and several people have been killed by bushpigs. When following one after a shot be sure to have a gun with stopping power.

Both warthog and bushpig are common throughout Southern Africa and many areas offer fine hunting for them.

CHAPTER 7

WATER CREATURES

This is where the species and experiences really begin to get interesting.

CROCODILE

The Nile crocodile is one of the biggest reptilian species in the world. He gets upwards of 15 feet long and up to 2000lbs in weight. He is of the dinosaur age and his whole being is made up of survival and killing. He is at the top of the food chain. A crocodile is made for and is adapted to be the ultimate predator. They have the patience of Job and will spend days stalking his prey if necessary. One of his many attributes is the ability to slow his heart rate to one beat per minute to allow him to remain underwater for ages. The crocodile has an amazing immune system with its own internal antibiotics for healing itself. Scientists believe there is much to be learnt still from these amazing creatures. Crocs are common throughout Southern Africa and will occur in any piece of water where they are not subject to persecution by man. In some of the wilder places like the Luangwa River and parts of Lake Kariba there are thousands of crocs, and one must pay serious attention when near water. Quick swims to cool off are like jumping train tracks - one wrong move or choice, and you become crocodile food. Do not just take a dip in ANY water unless you are very sure there are no crocs there. A croc can also move overnight, so be aware.

The crocodile must be one of the hardest species to take with a bow and arrow, and they are hard to recover. A well-placed arrow sends a croc boiling into the water, blood pumping out everywhere and he goes into death throes and dies. Sounds great right? The only minor problem is that they sink! And their blood will attract others. My wife and kids are not too keen on the idea of me diving for trophies in crocodile-infested waters!

On a hunt a couple years ago, a client shot a croc in the heart with his arrow. The croc dove in the Zambezi River and disappeared in a swirling

42

pool of blood. I really felt from experience that the croc was lost. While looking around, I wandered about 30 yards downstream where the bank rose sharply. I climbed to the top of this and looked around and, with my Costa del Mar Polaroids, I got a glimmer of white some nine feet deep. The croc had died and rolled belly up. We managed to hook him and bring him up - this was a real stroke of luck. Most waters are not clear enough to see more than three feet down.

A good crocodile for us is 12 - 14 feet. Over that is huge. These crocs will weigh between 1,200lb and 2,000lbs. The biggest a client took with me was 17 feet 6 inches - this was with a rifle. My friend, Steve Kobrine, shot a fourteen-and-half footer with his bow while on safari with me. Being so large and aggressive, the Nile crocodile is not like an alligator where you can stick him with a fishing bow and arrow and pull him in! It has taken me many experiences and hunts to finally have fine-tuned a method to take crocs with a bow. This is still not 100% but is the best I know.

A croc is cold blooded and can take a long time to die with a partial shot. Generally, when wounded, he will move to the edge of the water and will act differently - only experience can show you this.

I have found that if you can shoot a croc right through the line of four to five big round scales in the center of his body, it is generally successful. These scales are the last line of armor-type scales that cover a croc's back - please see my diagrams here and in the shot placement chapter. The lungs of a croc are like long tubes lying either side of the body on a lateral line. Those scales mark the shot for us. Place your arrow here and that croc will dive into the water at the shot. Try to set up so you are not shooting down but horizontally at your croc. If you can hit both lungs, this really helps. Bows should be 70lbs or more with a 450gr+ arrow.

His lungs will begin to fill with water and in seconds he will come to the surface with mouth open, and head for the bank. Just leave him there for as long as you can and let him die. This can take thirty minutes or three hours!

The best way to hunt a croc is to bait him or to set a pop-up blind near his sunning bed. When you do this, the wind has to be right, and I love a pop-up because a croc has brilliant eyesight. You must try to set yourself up in an area where, when the shot is taken, you can watch for the croc. It does not help if he has swamp or reeds or thick cover nearby because he will obviously head for that and disappear forever!

If you are setting bait on a river, throw lots of guts and blood in the water to attract crocs from downstream. Often you will have to chum a place gently with small pieces of meat and guts to get a croc used to a feeding site. I like to scout and find a big croc in the water or on the bank and then set up my bait as near as possible to him. You need to choose a spot that affords the croc a good approach (fairly deep water) and then rises to a shallow flat. It is best to stake a large piece of meat on this, so the croc's vitals are exposed but his belly is still wet. He will feel safe being close to deep water. I feel this all helps to bring them out in good time as opposed to in the dark!

In some areas that are populated with local people, the crocs tend to get harassed pretty badly and this renders baiting almost useless. At times like this, I like to set up a goat and, if you can bear it, a village dog is amazing. The idea is to stake them (without hurting them) in the same way as you

would dead meat. It needs to be done in such a way that the croc cannot just grab it and go. He must have to expose himself slightly for a shot before he can kill the animal. This is very hard to do and I would seriously advise you be sure you are experienced with doing this and how to do it. If not, the goat or dog will be snaffled, and you will have a really large price tag added from the person who loaned you his prize animal.

When hunting croc in this way, be sure to get local knowledge on your side. The fishermen will know where the big boys hang out and where they often attack people and livestock. Bear in mind that to the local people all crocs are monsters, so be prepared to do some scouting and be disappointed often. But you will eventually find a big one.

I have had many successful hunts using these methods now but have also still lost some crocs with guys in situations I cannot explain to this day. However, I have not had anyone come up with a better idea, so will keep using my method.

Crocodile meat is delicious if taken from the tail of a smaller croc, say between three and five feet. As a croc gets older he stores more and more fat in his tail. The meat becomes so rich that it is impossible to eat. Many African tribes believe that crocodile meat is poisonous. This can be understood as in Africa, nothing is wasted. Everything is cooked and eaten. The guts, meat and bones all go into the pot. The gall bladder of a croc is supposed to be toxic and there is definitely a toxin in the spinal column. So you can imagine how through history the story has evolved: The hunter kills a croc, proceeds to hack it all up to transport easier (thus getting toxins everywhere) and takes it to his village for a huge feast; everyone gets sick or, worse still, dies and the legend evolves: crocs are poisonous!

Finding a big croc is hard, baiting a croc is hard, setting up for croc is hard, shooting a croc is hard - this all leads to one conclusion - hunting a crocodile is a tough proposition with bow and arrow, and please be aware of this before you go on your croc hunt!

HIPPO

Hippos are huge animals that live on grass alone. They weigh somewhere in the region of 2.5 to 3 tons and have a bad attitude. Not part of the Big Five - hippos deserve to make up the Big Six.

The hippo is attributed with being the biggest killer of man in the mammal kingdom of Africa each year. Sadly, this is embellished a little bit by facts something like this: A dugout canoe carrying five people goes over the head of a resting hippo under the water. They are making a racket and it obviously

would irritate the hippo. He automatically will defend himself and attack the intruders and flip the flimsy craft. He may bite one or two people, but the rest drown and he, of course, is blamed for them all.

Because hippos live under water a lot of the time, people get too close without knowing it. Get five people together and all try to walk up to six or seven feet from an elephant - see what happens!

Hunting hippos is tricky in that they are nocturnal. Most areas do not allow hunting at night. During the day, hippos stay in the water but will come out to bask. Or they will lie half in the water with enough sticking out for a shot. A hippo's lungs sit very high up in the chest cavity for buoyancy purposes. This is great for a bowhunter as it offers a shot when not much else is sticking out of the water. Again - get it through to the lungs and the hippo will get out of the water. The great thing with hippo is that even with a good heart shot killing him quickly in deep water, there is no risk of losing your hippo. This large ruminant is always full of grass and consequently, gas. Thus he swells up like a balloon and will float.

Hippo are very territorial and bulls will defend this to the death. This makes patterning them easier. Hunting a hippo is a stalking game and is best done during the day as he suns himself or early in the morning as he returns to water along a trail from the night's grazing expedition. Be careful when hunting hippo on land. Often, if you get fairly close and he sees you , he will attack without hesitation.

We were walking along a riverbank one morning, looking for tracks when we crossed a relatively thick patch of bush and grass. When entering these places, as a PH my senses are always on high alert. This was a good thing that day because a hippo charged out of a thick patch about 15 yards from us. When I fired my .458 he collapsed no more than three feet from us.

Totally unprovoked and not wounded, this bull just decided we were in his space. I still wear the hippo skin bracelet which I was given by the local tracker for saving his life that day! The bracelet is slipped onto your wrist wet and then shrinks and dries – it is on forever unless cut off!

The hippo's nose and ears look cute, but his eyesight is not great. Once a hunting group and I walked up on a hippo bull lying in a pool in the Luangwa Valley. My client wanted buffalo and hippo, so we decided to have a look at this bull on Day 1 of a 10-day safari. We were about thirty yards away on a fairly raised bank with a bit of cover, looking at and filming the bull. In an instant, the bull stood up, swung round, and boiled up the bank toward us. I had no clear shot and my client had left the building! He was some 10 yards behind me and crouching to face the bull. I shouted for him to shoot. He had a .458 rifle, and I had my trusted .470 Nitro Express back-up rifle. As the bull got about six feet from me, I fired. Not knowing this, my client had stepped to the side and had fired at the same instant - both our bullets hit between the bull's eyes and he collapsed, like praying in front of

me! This was a rifle hunt, but my point here is that when approaching a hippo bull close, like with a bow and arrow, be extremely cautious - they will attack on a whim. I have had this happen more than once.

To kill a hippo successfully, I believe you should be shooting a 80lb bow rigged with AT LEAST an 850-grain arrow. Many believe that 70lbs is enough, which it is, if no rib is hit. Admittedly, the ribs on a hippo have very wide gaps between them. His defense here is more than two inches of skin over his chest area. But if you connect a rib, say goodbye to your great trophy, and you have a very dangerous animal wounded and which a PH should automatically back up and take out with a rifle. Not only is the hippo dangerous, but if he leaves his realm in search of a quiet place to hide and heal, it means moving up or down the river. Should a load of tourists on the opposite bank drive by and spot your hippo, the media world of today will have a field day with pictures of the arrow-stricken bull struggling along in the river. All because of hunters. This is how small mistakes have caused the ban of hunting dangerous game in many countries.

FISH

Bowfishing in Africa is perhaps not as big as in the USA, but if you know where to look, there is some amazing bowfishing to be had. South Africa has some wonderful lakes for great carp, barbel (a type of catfish), tilapia and other species of fish. I have spent a day on the water on a dam there, which was nonstop action the whole day! The boat was full of fish which were later donated to a local orphanage. From not using a finger tab, my fingers were raw and blistered, patched with band aids and my body was well tanned! Our biggest carp that day was about 25lbs!

When bowfishing, it normally takes several shots to compensate for refraction in the water. When you see a fish in the water, you must judge, according to its depth, how far in front of the fish to aim.

The water bends light and thus when your arrow enters the water it seems to bend towards the fish. If you do not compensate correctly you will shoot over the fish every time. A good pair of polarized sunglasses is absolutely imperative or there is no plan!

Here in Zambia, on certain rivers, if you chum the right place with a pile of lacerated intestines, you can bring in barbel and vundu. These are both catfish and barbel will get upwards of 30lbs and the vundu will get upwards of 80lbs. When you stick a big vundu you had better have top quality equipment because you are in for a hell of a fight! Tiger fish is another one that guys look for.

Vader bows are my choice of equipment for bow fishing.

CHAPTER 8

THE BIG GUYS

Here we cover the real bad boys of the large mammals in Africa. Buffalo, elephant and rhino are all part of the Big Five and take some serious nerve, top guiding, top equipment and precise shooting.

BUFFALO

The Cape buffalo is without a doubt one of the most sought-after trophies in Africa. Most hunters that get the Africa bug will have a Cape buffalo on their bucket list. The buffalo is a large, mean and take-no-BS animal. Big bulls will tip the scales at over 2,000lbs. Armed with hooves, deep curling horns and large bosses, a nasty temperament, and the ability to produce a gallon of adrenalin per hour, these animals are bad ass!

Buffalo are gregarious, and big herds may number over a thousand animals - truly a sight to behold and a sound to hear if you come across one of these. Bulls will live alone and form bachelor groups. These are the best options for a bowhunter as there are fewer eyes and ears. Their senses are all very sharp. Buffalo spend their lives being hunted by predators so they are built for defense. They will defend each other and protect each other fearlessly. Most buffalo occur in the big game concessions of Africa today. More and more are being bred on ranches now and are available to hunters. I personally believe that a ranch buffalo and wild buffalo are very different. Hunting both has shown me this.

To hunt a buffalo with a bow requires, in my opinion, a bow of no less than 80lbs. Arrows should weigh at least 850gr and if you can get them up to 1,000gr - even better. The arrow should be tipped with a good, strong broadhead. I like broadheads with two blades for the big game. I believe the heads made by Alaska Bowhunting and Sirius Archery Tuffheads are the best. These work great on buffalo, hippo, elephant and rhino.

A common misconception that many pro shops abroad give hunters, is that draw length, speed and a lighter arrow gets you plenty enough energy. However, consider the following: If you stood on an open field and were hit by a ping pong ball launched at you doing 250 feet per second, and then by a golf ball, also at 250fps, what do you think the result would be? Exactly - the ping pong ball would hurt and leave a mark. However, the golf ball doing the same, would likely kill you! The same principle applies to arrows. The heavier weight on your arrows gives you the biggest and often overlooked advantage - MOMENTUM. If you ever book a buffalo hunt, do yourself a favor - take my advice and ensure your total arrow weight with the broadhead sits around 750gr or more. It makes all the difference between a prick or a killing heart-stabber!

Buffalo can be hunted at water from a tree stand or ground blind, but often they will circle a waterhole before coming in to check for lions, etc.

The best and ultimate way to hunt a buffalo is to cut their tracks early in the morning and track them. In Africa, we have amazing trackers who will follow these tracks with ease. Your PH will know where to look and more than likely focus on areas where the buffalo would drink in the early hours. As I mentioned, following a bachelor group of Dagga Boys is the best option. Dagga is an African word for mud. Old bulls will roll in mud, often completely covering their hides with it to protect them from bugs. Hence their name – "Dagga Boys."

Once tracks are found, it must be ascertained from various factors, how far ahead they are and if it is worth following them. Tracking can take a couple hours walking to following all day, so have lots of water and be prepared for some tough hiking.

The trackers will normally advise you when you are getting close, and at this point, getting your wind right is very important. You ideally want to stalk your buffalo while they are still grazing. This means their heads are mostly down and they are busy filling their guts before they bed down for the day. Once your wind is right and you can see the buff and you know the direction they are heading in, you want to flank them and move into a position for a shot. All the while, test and keep your wind favorable. Set up so that you are well concealed and have a shooting lane for shots anything from 20 yards – 40 yards. Don't wait to shoot him at 10 yards as this will often lead to your detection up close and result in a turn and charge scenario - not good! Aim at his vital triangle - note where I shot my bull below. The second arrow was for penetration tests.

A buffalo is one of the most tenacious, toughest, and meanest of the Big Six animals. He does not die easily, but with a perfect arrow, and he could be dead in 40 yards. Yet another perfect arrow and he keeps going 10 minutes! A bad arrow, and he goes forever and becomes what could turn into your worst nightmare. If you blow a shot and you wound your buffalo - be sure to ask your PH to back you up. The buffalo will die eventually, but how many people could get hurt or killed in the follow-up process? Worse still, if you never see him again - who else could be hurt or killed by your animal?

One of my mentors in my hunting career once said to me "There are OLD hunters and there are BOLD hunters. However, there are no OLD, BOLD HUNTERS!"

How right he was. Take your time, pay attention, and take no stupid risks, and you will keep yourself and others safe.

I have hunted and guided so many buffalo hunts (literally hundreds), that I have seen a lot, and my stories are so many I would not know where to start. I have been chased into rivers, charged by wounded buffalo, charged when one was in a bad mood, been stampeded, and had my truck rammed. The list is endless.

I have had many hunts. To make it seem simple without a single mishap sometimes, it's best to just go easy.

When I mentioned stampedes… A client and I moved in on a herd of about 900 animals. The wind was good and we stalked up to a small mound with some shrubs and trees on it. The buffalo were spread out for about half a mile in front of us. We sat and watched cows and calves and bulls feeding around us for 40 minutes. Finally a big old bull with good drops and solid bosses came sauntering towards us. He was going about feeding and checking on the animals in his section of the herd. At 34 yards, he turned broadside and begun to work a small shrub with his horns. This was our window. My client settled into the shot and launched his arrow, sending it perfectly behind the shoulder. The bull lurched and turned and came boiling in our direction! He had no idea we were there but was hurt and now heading for the closest cover. From experience, I knew that if he came close and saw us, it would get

messy! He blew past us by about 14 yards and luckily we had made like a tree trunk by that stage! More worrying was the huge sound of thundering hooves of some 900 buffaloes following the bull's lead and bearing down in our direction! The PH, client, two trackers and government scout fast became at one with nature and up to the highest limb possible.

The local fellas climb incredibly well so they had no problem. By the time I had pushed and shoved my client up, I had just swung up when the first buffalo went by a mere two feet under me. We climbed higher! Thanks to someone up above, we had a few big trees in which to seek refuge. Had there only have been shrubs there - we would have been gored or trampled to death for sure. They thundered under us for about 25 minutes. The noise was deafening, the heat stifling and the dust unbearable. After almost an hour, things had simmered down and our bull lay about 90 yards away, stone dead. Huge trails had gouged themselves out on either side of him as the herd had galloped past. A lesson is here for anyone hunting large herds of buffalo - bear this in mind.

I hunted another bull once that a client made a perfect shot on from 18 yards. As the arrow buried into his heart, the bull turned instantly and came right at us. He must have known we were there or purely charged the noise of the bow. I had to shoot this bull or he would have got us. They are capable of covering enough ground, getting to you and killing you before they die - even from a heart shot!

When following a group of buffalo, always be on high alert. When a herd of buffalo feeds, the animals cover a startling amount of ground while doing so. They are constantly on the move. Old, sick and wounded animals do their best to keep up but ultimately fall behind - especially if you have bumped the herd and pushed them a little. These animals can surprise you and are extremely dangerous. They are likely to choose a thick spot to stop and rest. When you come bumbling past , the animal rushes you at an angle from behind and the PH has too many people in the hunting party between him and the buffalo to get a shot off. Bad news.

I was following a big herd of buffalo of about 500 animals late one evening. We had bumped the herd a final time and I decided to call it a day. We were walking back on a line to my hunting truck and were going through an area the buff had moved through. Fortunately, I am always aware of this possible danger and am constantly watching every patch of vegetation we go near. As we skirted a pretty bad spot,

I froze the whole group after spotting a sweeping horn in the undergrowth. As i focused on the bull and beckoned rapidly for everyone to "back up" he had had enough and came at us like a freight train. The client and scouts were off. With speed. The camera man did not even have time to press record! The buff bull had been wounded by lions and was clearly in pain. He saw us as a threat and it took him a split second to bust out of that cover and cover 20 yards to the nine paces where I shot him with my .470 back-up rifle!!

If you have Africa in your veins and have not hunted the Cape buffalo, seen him look down his nose at you with the, "you owe me money look," and taken up the tracks early in the morning – you really need to get on a buffalo safari. If you cannot draw a bow heavy enough, use a crossbow. If you won't use a crossbow, use a rifle. If none of these apply to you, at least accompany a buffalo hunter once. I promise you that it is well worth it.

ELEPHANT

The African elephant is the largest land mammal on earth and is truly the greatest challenge a bowhunter will ever encounter should he wish to hunt one. Not only is it a tough hunt, but your equipment HAS to be capable of killing an elephant. There is a huge amount of controversy over hunting elephant with bow and arrow. Sadly, due to many bad hunters' inconsideration, the hunting of elephant with bow and arrow is banned in many countries.

This is understandable as so many guys have come out to Africa with equipment capable of killing an elephant. But this is only if the shot is lucky enough to miss a rib. So, it really is a 50/50 deal. The PHs guiding these hunters, in my opinion, are more to blame as they should know what they are doing. If a client is ill-equipped, do not take him to shoot an elephant! It is as simple as that.

I believe that if a client is not shooting a bow of 80lb or more, and if he does not have an arrow weighing more than 900gr and a broadhead with only two edges, then he is not ready nor capable of hunting elephant. In my opinion the 300gr Ashby and 300gr Tuffhead are the best broadheads for this job. Notably, both heads are single bevels. I know that pro shops around the world will be booing me right now but I feel very strongly about this. I feel I have seen enough hunts to be able to comment on the subject at length.

An elephant is hunted on your feet and killed with your equipment. Be prepared mentally and physically for an elephant hunt. You will most likely spend many days following tracks before you find your trophy. A typical day on an elephant hunt will start very early. I will take a client to likely elephant country and begin covering the ground with a truck until we cut fresh sign from in the night. The best place to look is along roads adjacent to rivers, water points, or riverbeds. Once we find tracks, I decide whether it is a good bull or not and if it is worth following. Typically, any back foot track that is longer than 22 inches long is worth a look. This will of course vary from area to area.

Should we find a group of bull tracks, I will look through them with my trackers. Often a big old bull will be protected by several "askaris" or body guards as we know them. The old bull's track can be recognized by worn-smooth back edges, have deep cracks in his feet, and his dung pile may contain unchewed sticks and leaves – this is a good indicator of an old elephant with no teeth left.

Once I decide we are going to follow the tracks, our gear is put together. We will always have a first aid kit, lots of water and sometimes even a food pack. Elephants cover amazing distances, particularly in areas where they are hunted regularly. They know of the imminent danger from man after watering. When a bull is on the move, we have to take seven paces to his every one! Tracking is an art, and it still baffles me how a seven-ton mammal and four feet can just vanish without a trace or sound!

Elephant have great hearing and brilliant smell but their eyesight is bad. As the distance with an elephant closes, you will notice that his poop piles get warmer and warmer. There is normally plenty of this to test! An elephant will drink up to 100 liters and eat up to 600lbs of vegetation daily. They need to poop!

Once I feel we are getting close, the trackers and I become on high alert for the sound of breaking branches as the elephant try to get to the highest and sweetest browse. If it is still early, the bull or bulls are likely to be feeding and this is a very audible giveaway to their position. If it is later in the day, we are constantly on the look ahead for likely areas where an old bull would stop and rest through the hot hours.

Once we are aware of where the elephant are, things get serious. At this time, silence and the wind is imperative. Get the wind right and move in very slowly. I will even approach in socks or bare foot if the terrain allows. I like to know exactly where each elephant is before closing the gap completely. Always remember, once you are in their safety circle, it becomes very dangerous. Do not close with elephants for fun – only do it if you are sure there is a trophy bull there that you intend to kill. It is not worth getting in a pickle because of a wind shift and ending up with your tag being used by the PH killing your elephant in self-defense or, worse still, a smaller askari! The younger askaris will protect their old leader aggressively. I like to get my client into a shooting lane with about 25-30 yards between us and the elephant. **There are two reasons for this**.

1. If you are very close, the elephant will react to the bow shot and often spin and charge that direction – means I must kill it!
2. It allows that stiff and heavy arrow a little time to stabilize and fly straight as can be. A wobbly arrow at impact causes a huge loss of penetration as the energy is lost in the sideways flick of the arrow as it enters the animal.

I also like to have a large tree, or bush, or boulders or a downward slope as cover. This will generally send your arrow-struck bull away from you. If you are in the open and he can locate your position from the bow shot, that bull becomes aware of you when you send an arrow into his body – and he will most likely attack his aggressor. Then a rifle has to come into your hunt.

One day a client and I watched a bull doze under a tree for over three hours. We stood in the sun next to a fallen tree with nowhere to go. The bull was slightly quartered toward us and we could not move. We were incredibly lucky that the wind allowed this. The old bull eventually shifted his position and allowed us a heart shot.

My point here is that you must not shoot unless that elephant is exactly broadside, and you have a perfectly clear shooting lane. Those heavy arrows

have a massive trajectory arc and overhanging limbs are a problem. I tell my clients to follow the crease up behind the front leg until it ends. Then take a wide hand space forward from there. An arrow placed here is into the heart and often misses the ribs. I have had 100% success with shots placed here. An elephant must be struck in the heart with an arrow if you want a good, clean, bow kill. Bear in mind that your arrow has about two feet of muscle, skin and possibly rib before it even reaches the first lung. Ideally, I like to see an arrow disappear into this spot to be sure of a clean kill. If your arrow buries well here, you are sure of a good kill on your elephant.

In my early days of hunting elephants with a bow, I had a client with bow

set at 85lbs and with 850gr arrows (less than I will allow today). We had come up on two bulls that were known crop raiders. As we closed the gap, our wind shifted and the bull we intended to shoot became very agitated. He began advancing on our position and so I pulled us out of there. Just as I thought we were clear, the bull came – it seemed he was following our scent on the ground! We quickly ran and as we went I noticed a gully to our right. We ran along this until we reached a large trail that elephant would use to cross the ditch. We crossed this and quickly broke left with and across the wind. I stopped by a large bush 27 yards away and prepared my client. At this point, my client informed me that I was totally nuts!

Inevitably, the bull followed. As he entered the gully, he stopped in the river sand to sniff around. My client had his bow drawn and ready. The bull turned slightly, still scenting, and I told my client to shoot. The arrow was perfect and disappeared into the elephant on the magic spot. The bull spun and took off down the gully bed roaring. He had gone about 80 yards and came crashing to a halt in a cloud of dust and debris.

On inspecting the carcass later, I found it had been wounded by villagers with muskets and my client's arrow had passed between the ribs and went right through the heart to stop on the other side. Great shot, quick kill – what every hunter wants.

But if he had hit a rib, it could have been a mess because there is no way that arrow would have got through. I have since learned that lesson!

Many hunters have hunted elephant cows. They are smaller and a bit easier to kill. I believe that hunting elephant cows is one of the most dangerous hunts you can go on. They are very aggressive and protect each other to the death. If a PH offers to take you on an elephant cow hunt – be VERY sure you are aware of his capabilities for hunting dangerous game, and elephant in particular. This is not for the faint-hearted and often ends in very tricky situations with elephants being shot in self-defense. Please be careful. I have had many cases of having to run for our lives from elephant cows, and several cases of having to shoot cows in a last-minute moment of self-defense.

Some clients and I were walking back from following a buffalo herd one day. As the truck became visible in the distance, my tracker who had stayed with the vehicle motioned to his right and made us aware of about seven elephant cows with calves resting under a large tree some 250 yards off. As we approached closer, trunks went up and they apparently got our wind. The whole herd became very agitated and advanced toward us. They started screaming and picking up the pace and the evasive maneuver began! We ran hard. I asked the scout to fire a shot in the air from his AK47. He did. The herd became even angrier! We ran some more. I asked him to fire again. His gun had jammed. He was off, left us all in the dust! Bear in mind this is all happening at a full run.

I got my trackers to take a client each and keep moving ahead and away as safely as possible. I chose a large tree with a huge trunk to make my stand. Double in hand, bullets wedged in fingers for reloading and me screaming at the top of my lungs - I stood my ground and prepared for battle or certain death!

I drew an imaginary line at about 12 yards in front of me and started mentally preparing for a series of brain shots on any elephant that crossed it. The whole herd stopped and fanned at about 15 yards with the obvious matriarch standing at the head, screaming back at me. I had my front bead trained between her eyes, screaming, "don't make me f**%#^~ kill you!"

After what seemed like an eternity, there was a silent stalemate and they all turned and rumbled off. I had about pooped my pants!

It was one of those rare moments in life that turned out so much better than it really could or would have.

RHINO

Hunting white rhino is only possible in South Africa and Namibia. Now and then a permit is released for a black rhino hunt in Namibia. Your equipment needs to be the same as for elephant, and no less. Their ribs are often thicker than that of an elephant. A new and very popular way of doing a rhino hunt is by putting a tranquilizer dart on your arrow. The animal is hunted and is shot like normal; it is then set up for your pictures and then a vet will wake it up and let it go. Your trophy is an exact replica made of synthetics.

Both the black and white rhino have great noses and ears but terrible eyesight. They are hunted by tracking, much the same as with elephants. The black rhino is very aggressive and will attack on impulse. The white is more docile. That does not mean to say they are not dangerous.

All these big, thick-skinned animals have a considerable element of danger surrounding them. Please make sure you have an experienced PH and are well equipped before you go after them. It is important for other hunters and for the lives of the people around you.

GIRAFFE

These animals are huge, and you need equipment equal to your buffalo or, even better, your elephant rig. Many hunters will kill a giraffe with a frontal shot between the legs. This is easily done with lower poundages, but the shot must be precisely between the shoulder ball joints. The broadside shot needs to be placed very high up on the giraffe's body. Be sure that your PH explains this to you. The other tough part of hunting giraffe with a bow is the fact that he can see you from a mile away with his height advantage. Many are shot at waterholes from a blind.

CHAPTER 9

SMALL CRITTERS

This chapter covers the minor predators like jackal, caracal, serval, genet and civet cat. All these little critters are nocturnal and are normally hunted at night and on private property. I like to have my plains-game bow rigged with a stabilizer light of some kind that I can switch on when I am at full draw and ready to shoot.

JACKAL AND CARACAL

The best way to hunt a jackal is at a bait, or to call him in with a predator call. A pop-up blind with shooting windows all around is very useful for this. With a good dying-rabbit call or jackal call, they will run right into you. I know several hunters have taken jackal from blinds at waterholes.

I sat by a natural waterhole one day from first light till dark. I knew of a big old waterbuck that hung about there and I wanted to hunt him. I got to my spot before light and set up under some shrubs on a mound with a good view of the pan. My wind was good, and I waited. And waited! That old waterbuck was smarter than me! Right about last light, I was numb, bored and knew every inch of that pan by heart! Then I caught a movement to my left and there came a jackal. I figured that if I could shoot him without a blind – I would. As he passed behind a bush I drew my bow. The jackal came round and was on to me. He clearly felt something was up and froze, looking right at me. I guess he felt if he did not move, I would not see him.

The other species I have mentioned are normally taken by luck at a bait or while riding around for hours at night with a lamp. If you truly want to collect the small cats – there are several outfitters in South Africa that sell hunts over hounds. They will tree your little cat and you must then make an upward kill shot.

CHAPTER 10

BIG CRITTERS THAT WILL
BITE YOU BACK!

This chapter covers the main predators - hyena, cheetah, leopard, and lion. A bow of no less than 60lbs is recommended for these animals. Broadheads should have a good cutting diameter like 1½ inch plus, and MUST be brand-new and razor sharp. Hyena are extremely tough. The cats die easily as long as the arrow is perfect and the sharp broadhead is able to cut a clean wound channel.

If the arrow is bad, you have a very, very serious situation on your hands. Predator hunts are what I call "set piece hunts". Everything about the setup must be perfect and fine-tuned to the last detail so that when a client releases his arrow – it is hard for him to miss.

HYENA

To hunt a hyena with a bow is a considerable challenge. They are very secretive and wily creatures. In some African tribes, it is believed that the hyena is a reincarnated witch, and they are highly respected and feared as such. Hyenas are known as being predominantly scavengers. However they are very effective and successful hunters in their own right.

The best way to hunt a hyena is to bait him. A large bait placed on the ground is a key factor to ensure he is kept busy all night without finishing it. The bait must, of course, be secured with chain or wire to prevent the hyena from pulling it away. Try and set up your bait so that you can build your blind in such a way as to have the wind in your face and some sort of physical back stop to prevent the hyenas coming from behind you, such as a mountain, river, ditch or something similar. Personally, I love using a pop-up blind for all my predator hunting!

Let the hyenas feed for the first night and then be sure to be sitting there on night two ready for them at last light. Again, most safari areas do not allow the use of lights, so last light and early morning is your best option. It is considerably easier if you are allowed to use a light, like on many private properties.

If you happen to find a dead elephant or hippo or buffalo during your safari, this is a perfect place to set up for hyenas – just pay attention. There could also be lions playing on that carcass and they are a little more possessive of meat than hyenas!

I shot a hyena once from 35 yards frontal. The arrow went through him at more of an angle than I expected. We tracked him well into the next day

and when I found him, he wanted to eat us, and he was shot in a charge! My arrow had gone clean through one lung and he was still strong as an ox! The hyena had survived the whole night and traveled some six miles before we caught up with him.

In the case of problem animal control, i.e. hyenas that are killing livestock, a hunter may be allowed to use a call. This is a very effective and exciting method of hunting hyenas. They come boiling in looking for a fight and it is a real rush. Again, be sure you have an experienced guide when doing this. Hyenas are big and can be aggressive – they fight lions and leopards the whole time, so are capable of holding their own.

CHEETAH

Hunting the cheetah is also a tough proposition because they will not come to bait or call. Added to this, the only place they can be hunted legally is in Namibia and even these trophies are not allowed back into the USA.

The only way to hunt a cheetah with a bow is to find out from your guide where a male is regularly seen. A male is easy to distinguish by his genitals at the back under his tail. You then have to find what is called a "scratching tree." Cheetahs will return often to certain trees and scratch the trunks as a way of marking their territories. Find one of these scratched-up trunks and set your pop-up blind 30-40 yards downwind and spend some time there. After that, it is all luck! Place the arrow behind the shoulder and the cat will be yours.

Cheetah can be aggressive but nothing in the class of lion and leopard.

LEOPARD

The beautiful leopard is one of my favorite hunts. These cats are one of the most magnificent creatures on earth. They are smart, adaptable, strong, and extremely dangerous when wounded, making them earn a respectable place in the Big Five. Contrary to popular belief, leopard is one of the most successful predators in Africa and they are widespread, even living in several African cities with an abundant food supply of stray dogs and cats!

Leopards are brilliantly successful hunters and are true masters in the art of stalk and ambush attacks on prey of their choice. However, they are not shy to cash in on a free meal should the opportunity present itself.

We hunt a leopard by hanging a well-chosen bait (meat he cannot resist) in a tree to lure him in. The preference of bait varies from area to area, but a few are always sure winners for me, certain favorites being hippo, zebra, donkey, impala, and baboon. Hunting a leopard is an art and I believe some hunters have the knack and some just don't. It requires a true understanding of the cat and his habits and tendencies. It is necessarily a set piece hunt. In other words, every little detail has to be perfect so that when

that leopard arrives, the person drawing the bow is in a position that gives them a more than average chance of making a clean kill.

First, you need to know of the presence of a nice male in the area you wish to hunt. A hunter will know this from finding regular tracks of a male. Males are bigger than females and will have a large pair of nuts protruding from under his tail. If he's got these, you are onto a nice tom cat.

Next, a suitable tree needs to be selected to hang your bait in. I like to find a tree with a good leaf cover if possible, to help hide the bait from vultures, and be adjacent to good cover where I know the leopard can go and lie up

and feel safe for the day. I also like the bait tree to be close enough to cover that can conceal him well, which will make him more comfortable to come to the bait in daylight hours. I always bear in mind the prevailing wind direction so as to have the bait scent blowing toward me. You also want your bait set up within reasonable distance of water as the cat will build up a thirst whilst feeding.

Please bear in mind that if you are in an area that has a lot of elephants, they also like to hit the water in the late evening and can be a danger to you in a blind! Don't set your blind up on an elephant trail! Setting the bait is important. I like to use steel chain with a clip or heavy-gauge wire to hang my meat out of reach of lions and hyenas. (I once saw a trail cam with over 1000 pictures of a jumping hyena – he jumped all night long, determined to get that meat.) Be sure the chain or wire goes around a solid bone in your bait or the cat will break the bait away, steal the meat and never come back.

To ward off the possibility of vultures, I make a skirt out of grass which is wrapped around the meat. Any vulture that lands on it will have no grip, slide off and get bored. Also, throw gut content and blood all over the areas you have worked to act as an attractant and to mask human scent.

I like to put a trail cam on every bait – this allows you to see exactly what comes to your bait and also gets you some amazing wildlife-in-action pictures! It is always such fun checking baits in the morning – you find

yourself trying to bend your head around corners to see if you have a hit on a bait you are approaching. You then cannot wait to download the trail-cam pics, all part of the hype and fun of a great hunt!

A bait is good until it is dripping maggots – leopard relish a piece of smelly, green meat but when it goes black, change for a fresh piece. Bear this in mind when you are setting up your baiting routines. You do not want to leave a bait tree with no meat in it for any amount of time. You may miss that monster coming to have a look! Meat will normally last seven to ten days, depending on your daily temperatures and time of year.

I like to use a pop-up blind to hunt from. It is quiet to set up, quick to brush in to prevent disturbance around the bait, and the cats cannot see you in them. I have had several instances of leopards looking into the blind mere feet away and just carrying on as normal! In my opinion, every hunter should use one when hunting a leopard. Set your blind up no more than 25 yards from the bait. I like a 15 - 20 yard shot. If the bait is at 15 yards or closer, be sure to shoot your bow at this range to see if your pin is set right.

As soon as you have a good hit on your bait by a male, be sitting and ready in your blind by 4.30 the following evening. I like to hunt the evenings only as I firmly believe it is impossible to approach and enter a blind 20 yards from the bait in the early hours of the morning without the leopard knowing

exactly what you are doing. He will have been there and close to his meat all night. Disturbing the cat will educate him and you will most likely never see him in daylight after that.

Set up sturdy and comfortable chairs to wait in the blind. If you are allowed to use a light, then a good mattress and a pillow is better! Remember, you have to sit incredibly silently or he will hear you. I like to set the client's chair up side on to the shooting window with a nice clear shot. You always want to take an archery shot with bow shoulder pointing at the target… i.e. side on. If not, it may alter your anchor points and affect your shot. I do not like my guys shooting leopard on the bait branch because of the upward angle which guys tend to forget in the excitement. If they do not bend at the waist, the arrow goes high and the whole deal ends up with a very pissed-off high-shouldered cat that you will rarely find again. When we decide to sit for a particular cat, I like to tie a piece of meat to the base of the tree which the leopard always finds before climbing to the upper bait. When he goes to work on the lower piece of meat is when I want my client to draw his bow, take his time, and place that arrow halfway up right behind the shoulder.

This has worked really well for me and my clients.

There is nothing that can prepare you for when that leopard male of yours first appears! It is breathtaking and an adrenalin rush of note! It is good to watch the cat a while if you can. This will allow your nerves to settle a little before your shot. Leopard will often lie around under the bait, fighting off tsetse and other biting flies. They stretch and yawn. They will territory mark and scratch and pee on the dirt. A client of mine and I had one doing this so close to our blind once we were getting sprayed with sand and leopard piss! Once he is settled and comfortable, he will start to eat the bait – and now it is your turn to settle and to make the shot of a lifetime!

Take your time! You will have enough. Be 100% sure that your leopard is broadside on and in a standing position on all four feet before you shoot him. You will often get a cat sitting on his haunches with his body upright looking toward or away from you or even broadside, and it is so tempting to run him through. Trust me, it generally ends in tears and a wounded cat. Wait for him to be broadside and at the meat and eating.

An arrow behind the shoulder, center mass, will render your leopard dead within 50 yards. If he is not, prepare yourself for action because your shot was poor, and he is now really annoyed! If the cat is vaguely alert or jumpy – do not shoot. They are extremely fast and will attempt to jump the string, causing a possible wounded situation.

Every leopard hunt and area has its own differences and PHs have their ways of doing things. Choose yours well and then be patient. You are hunting one of the smartest creatures around and it can be trying and sometimes ends in failure but, generally, if you persevere, you will take one of the most amazing animals and memories hunting has to offer!

LION

The king of the jungle. This is a species that is generally taken at the pinnacle of a hunter's career. Today, hunting a wild lion has become extremely pricy and, as a result, has become out of reach of many hunters' budgets. I have been lucky enough to hunt several, and with those hunts have memories second to none. I truly believe that only once you have hunted a lion or been on a lion hunt, can anyone really understand how amazing these animals are.

There are many lions hunted on large ranches in South Africa and these hunts are good, but I am afraid that there is nothing like the challenge

and excitement, the highs and lows of a wild lion hunt. Lion numbers are still excellent in many countries – our numbers in Zambia are still great. Sadly, there is a lot of anti-hunting sentiment creeping in and putting pressure on our local governments. If only these green factions knew how much damage they were doing. With no value (and photographic is not value), our lions are being persecuted daily by local communities that are snaring, poisoning, and shooting lions to protect their livestock.

Hunting a big old six-year-plus male lion is a minimum of a 21-day affair. It needs to be done in a good safari area with decent numbers of resident lions. It takes lots of patience, a good PH and very sharp trackers with a fine knowledge of the area that is being hunted. To hunt a lion with a bow, you need bait meat - lots of meat. I like to use hippo – it will give you four really big, greasy and smelly baits that lion generally love. Elephant is good – especially if you find a whole dead one! Lions pick up that large scent trail from a long way off. Buffalo is good, as is a whole zebra or wildebeest, and kudu is often a favorite! You need to put the whole carcass out when it comes to zebras and kudus because if four males or a pride come along, they

will eat a whole zebra in one sitting. I strongly recommend that you either take a rifle with you or ensure your PH has a good , scoped rifle in camp so that you do not mess around with getting baits. You really cannot afford to be spending days trying to kill something for bait with a bow when you are hunting a lion!

A chain to tie your baits to the tree is a must. You will need a winch from your hunting truck to haul meat up. I like securing my meat at a height where a grown man standing reaches up and can touch the bottom of the hanging bait. This is to keep hyenas off but, more importantly, the lions will be able to eat most of the meat but not reach it all – this makes them return for more the following day. Like with leopard, if they finish or steal the meat – your cat is gone. Hang your meat in a tree that is hard to climb, and secure the chain around a major bone in your meat. Lions are generally poor climbers but if the tree is easy they will get up and finish off the bait. Saying all this, I once had a big male lion climb a tough tree, bite through the leg bone of a buffalo hindquarter and carry it away to a place of his choice. Sadly for him, my trackers were on their A-game and we tracked him down, and he now has a place of pride in a trophy room in Denmark! This is a valid point to remember, because if you ever get chased by a lion, don't believe you can climb a tree and be safe!

A bait tree must be fairly near water and preferably in an area where your PH or trackers know a big old male likes to wander or cruise his territory. A lion can cover 30 miles in a night. Once a tree is selected, I prefer my lion blind to be 30 yards away if it will be a pop-up. Many hunters just will not hunt on the ground for a lion – so if you have one of these PHs, your tree blind or machan can be closer. Lions can be very aggressive at a bait, and once the sun sets they truly become king and are scared of absolutely nothing! They will put their heads in blinds and they will defend their meat with vigor! Extra care needs to be taken if there are lionesses involved. I love hunting the evening and then getting my truck to come and pick us up 30 minutes after sunset. If I feel we need to spend the night in a blind for an early morning lion, then I will brush my blind in well with larger thorn branches. I always set my baits so that when I check them, I can drive almost right up. This will also allow the lion to get used to the truck for dropping us into the blind and

being picked up without too much disturbance. I learnt my lesson at the young age of 17. I went to check a bait for a PH and went alone. I got to about 30 yards of the bait and it looked like the area was clear. I went up to inspect the bait, and on a closer look realized that lions had been feeding up under the grass skirt. Not much was eaten, and this immediately led me to believe that the cats were close. I turned to the side slightly and our eyes locked! At this point, the rifleless young learner hunter broke at high speed for the truck! I could hear the lioness gaining on me fast – I entered the cab headfirst, with a very loud bang on the door from the lioness! I will never again approach bait from any distance without a weapon.

A trail cam is a wonderful tool to have. This will give you an exact idea of the sort, size and age of the lion you are dealing with. It also helps to get an idea of when he likes to feed.

If I get a good hit on a bait and I have pictures of what I feel are a shooter lion, then my client and I will be in the blind ready by 4 p.m. When a lion comes in, 99% of the time he will notice the blind. It does not mean anything other than there is something new there, and more than likely he will come right up and investigate it. When this happens, remain calm, let him come, do his thing, and whatever you do, DO NOT be tempted to shoot at six yards from the blind. By doing this, your arrow trajectory will be different and just might wound him. On top of this, that lion will now be fully aware of your presence, and it may cause him to join you in the blind, the outcome of which will not be in your favor! If you just sit and enjoy the moment, most times he will come and do his inspection, may roar or growl a bit at your scent, but generally he will return to his bait meat. When he is there, wait for him to turn broadside for your shot. Place your arrow center mass about six inches behind the shoulder crease. A lion's vitals sit back

in his body. Make sure he is not looking at you when you shoot him. Generally, when an arrow strikes a lion, he has no idea what has happened and just gets pretty pissed at this pain in his side. I have often had them expire within 20 yards of a bait. However, if he is looking at the blind, he will know where the pain came from. I once had

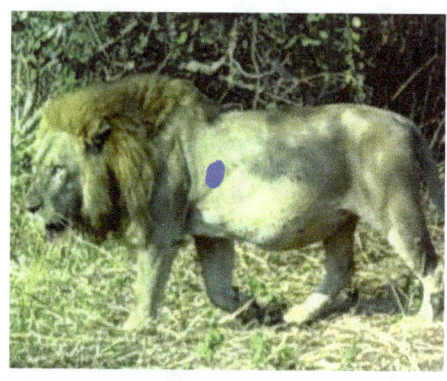

a client shoot a lion that was looking at us. That cat boiled down a bank straight for the blind. As I was about to shoot him with my .470, he turned and ran past the blind, spraying it with sand and blood! This was where I learnt to be sure that he is not looking at you when you let loose that arrow. That scenario could have gone horribly wrong.

Another thing to bear in mind with both lion and leopard – do not be tempted to shoot them when they are standing up and feeding. Their vitals are in a different position and all too often they are moving about while they feed. I have had a couple cases of these shots being bad. It kills the cat eventually but not as quick as a regular broadside shot. This is a case where your safari can go pear-shaped and someone can get hurt badly or, worse still – killed. As I keep saying and will always say, as bowhunters, we are constantly under pressure for being cruel, inhumane, and inefficient hunters. Please help us all by making the right shot choices and in doing so making us proud with quick, disturbance-free kills. It also goes a long way with the trackers out here!

In the case of problem lions, a caller may be allowed to be used. A caller is an amazing tool and very effective. But please, please, please be extremely careful how you use it. Lions, male and female alike can come in fast and with a serious amount of attitude – it is extremely dangerous. Especially with a bow.

I once had a cattle-killer come into me with a caller. Up until then, this lion had killed almost 30 cattle and two kids, and the government wanted me to take care of it, no matter what. I had hunted him for 30 days and only seen his track!

Now I was on the ground in a pop-up blind with windows all round me so I could shoot in any direction from which he came. I start calling at dusk and by the time he came it was dark and all I could hear was him hurtling to the blind. He went past at three yards, smelt me, bellowed out a roar and trotted off. Being alone in the blind (like an idiot) my nerves were now prickling with tension. Shortly after, I could hear him approach the blind

slowly. He lay next to the blind, began growling and messing with the brush I had used to cover the pop-up! At this stage, there was three feet and a canvas sheet between me and a large growling lion! And it was dark! I laid down the bow and picked up my .375 H&H. I shouted "HEY!"

at the cat, and with this he roared again and left. I had a flashlight mounted to my rifle barrel and I decided to try to get a look at the lion and possibly take a shot.

From where I last heard his low growl, I had no decent window so I leant out one of them at an angle, and left-handed I might add! I pushed the light switch to on and immediately saw a set of eyes come up at 25 yards or so. At that time he roared again and charged. I fired left-handed and, only being able to point, could not get over the scope from that angle. The light went off and it was silent, apart from my over adrenalin-filled, quivering body!

When my tracker and truck arrived, we found the lion stone dead at about 20 yards. My bullet had gone clean through the front paw (in the bound) and entered at the base of his throat, running him through and, thankfully, killing him instantly. The cattle-fed cat was huge – he weighed over 600lbs and had no mane. On closer inspection, a villager had dusted him with buckshot from a shot gun. He had nine holes in his butt. No wonder he was displeased!

CHAPTER 11

Basic illustrations of where shots should be placed on the various animal categories.

The following chapter has a few basic illustrations of where shots should be placed on the various animal categories. All my pictures also contain neck or hip or head-shot placements – these are for rifle hunter shots should there be an animal that you have wounded and don't want to lose. The archery shots are the ones indicated behind the shoulders. Always remember, folks – and it is a common mistake we all make too often – if you do not see your animal go down from your shot, wait at least 30 minutes. If you cover 100 yards and are not convinced of the shot – give it another 30 minutes. Many animals are lost by rushing the follow-up. I advise you – take this time. If it is down it is not going anywhere. If not, it may be marginal and needs some time. If you bump him, he may be lost forever and that is terrible. Experienced bowhunting PHs will know this.

Plains game – always aim to shoot right behind the shoulder, halfway up as tight to the shoulder crease as possible.

Buffalo – see illustration

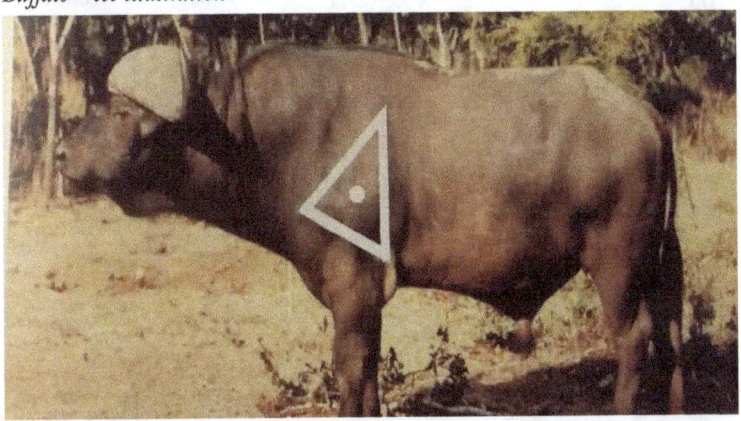

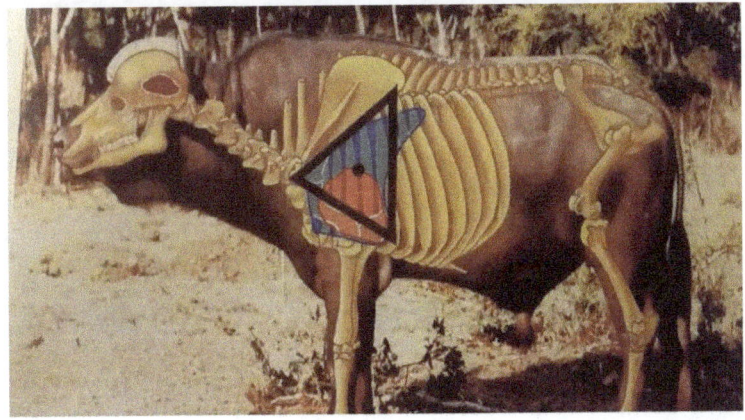

Hippo – see illustration. The lungs of a hippo sit very high in their bodies for buoyancy – if a foot is sticking out of the water – you have a shot.

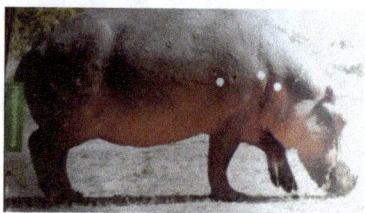

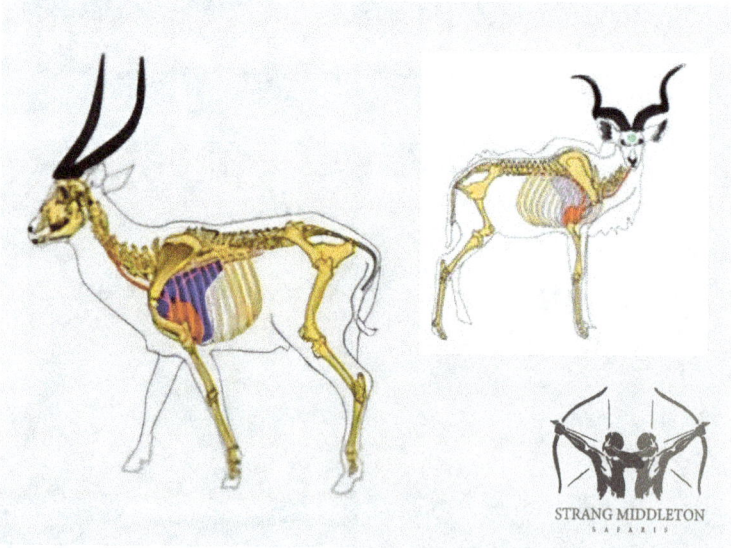

Elephant – always shoot an elephant broadside on and be sure to place your arrow a full hand-space forward of the top of the shoulder crease.

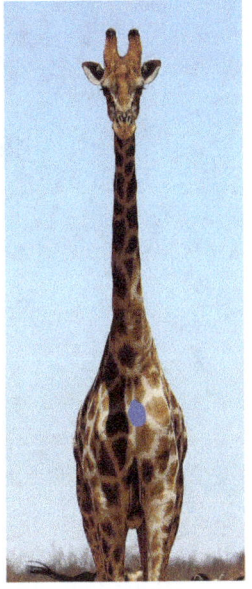

Giraffe – a high shot is needed to take these large animals down.

Crocodile – see illustration. It is hard to believe that mid-body is correct, but please trust me – this IS the area to shoot a croc.

Cats – bear in mind that a lion must be shot a little bit back – about six inches behind the shoulder.

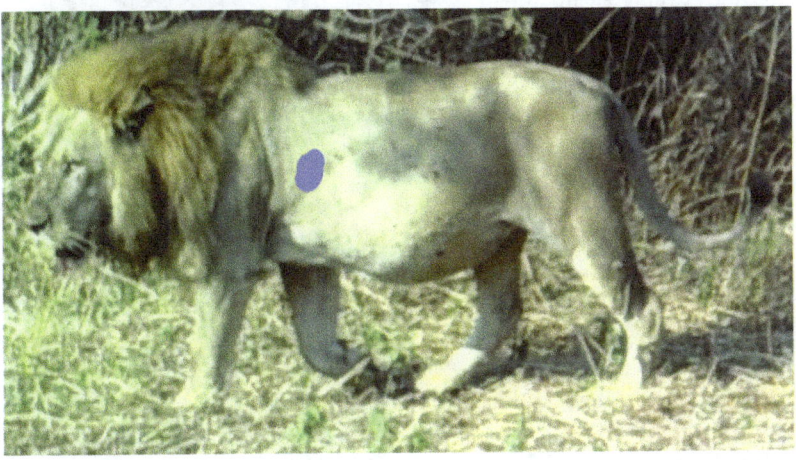

Very basically, an arrow kills by cutting – an arrow placed behind the shoulder of any animal broadside on is imperative. There are other shots that are brilliant, for example right in the middle of the rump. It will stop an animal. Of course, use this when you are trying to get a second arrow in an animal. Experienced hunters will know how to use a Texas heart shot and a frontal shot – these are very hard to master and not what you should try, except on a giraffe frontal shot. It also needs high poundage to achieve it.

CHAPTER 12

CAMO

This chapter covers a few of my preferred and advised choices of camouflage that have worked well for me over the years.

The idea with camo is to help break up your outline and to blend with your surroundings. The first thing to consider about Southern Africa is that our vegetation is generally green from December to May. Then your browns and greys come into effect the rest of the year. Check with your PH before you come over as to the vegetation colors during your trip. Many areas remain green year-round. I love a mix of brown, grey, green and black in my patterns.

When hunting from stands and by stalking, I think all the camos work fairly well – the biggest thing to remember is your face. This stands out like a lighthouse beacon! Be sure to paint or smudge it with darker colors. My opinion however, is that if we are trying to break our outline, then the very best and definitely my favorite type of camo is a leafy suit. These have worked the best for me. I have crawled right up to game with this. There is a theory by some that using anti-UV stuff works. I have not put it to the test yet!

Please note that military design camo is illegal in most African countries.

When it comes to scent-cover, this does work but, in Africa it is hot and really miserable if you bundle up with scent clothing. Added to this, if one arrow or one string silencer, or your release smells slightly funny – our animals will pick this up! There is only one proven 100% system – hunt into the wind and hunt it as slow as possible!

CHAPTER 13

WHAT TO TAKE ON SAFARI

Here we deal with a basic list of what I feel every client should be considering to take with him on his or her safari to Southern Africa. It is a guideline and I suggest you sit with your PH and discuss this list with him beforehand.

Medical – Be sure to have all your jabs and immunizations up to date, e.g., yellow fever jabs. Pack all your own personal medications/vitamins. Take a small pack of medications for flu, stomach problems, menstrual problems, headaches, stings and bites and minor cuts and grazes. Ask if you are travelling to a malaria area! Malarone is the best one to take for this. Also bring insect repellent (Avon Skin So Soft insect repellent is brilliant, even for tsetse flies!). Don't forget sunscreen and your basic toiletries. Ladies, please remember when that time of the month could arrive for you. I have had a couple of cases on safaris where women have forgotten all about this and when you are stuck in the middle of the bush on a 21-day safari, it can be a problem!

Clothes – Discuss this with your PH. Most camps will have a full laundry service so if you bring the following you will be fine: 2 x light trousers: 2 x light shirts: 2 x shorts: 3 x underwear: 3 x socks: 1 x warm jacket: cap, hat and beanie: whatever camo you decide on. For me: 2 x leafy suits and face paint: 1 x hunting boots: 1 x casual shoes or sneakers (can be used if boots get messed up): 1x slops/sandals: 1 x sunglasses.

Equipment – Your bow of choice for the hunt: 12 x arrows minimum: 12 x broadheads minimum: 2 x releases: 1 x Allen wrench: 1 x spare sight: 1 x range finder: 1 x binocular : 4 x field tips to practice: 1 x sturdy bow case: 1 x portable bow press if possible: 1 x spare peep sight: 1 x pop-up blind: 1 x good headlight or flashlight: possible rainwear.

I feel these are the very basics one needs. As I said, go through all of this with your PH before your trip.

CHAPTER 14

EXPECTATIONS

This chapter just covers a few of the basic things to expect on a hunt and what may be expected of you as the client. My hope is that it will make you just a little better prepared for a successful safari.

Any hunter planning a trip to Africa must be proficient with the weapons they intend to use. It does not help to come with an aggressive cam bow shooting arrows at blistering speeds if, all you have ever shot is a solo cam. Be sure to have practiced hard and be well familiar and confident with your equipment.

Try to get in as good a shape as you possibly can. This makes for a much easier hunt. Wear in those hunting boots before you come on safari - it does not help if you arrive with new boots, and after day one your blisters are so bad you cannot move. You would think that is obvious, but you will be amazed at how many people do just that!

Once you have chosen a PH – trust in him. He will do his best to give you a great hunt. Let him make the decisions and guide you. It is super frustrating to have a client telling you how to run a safari in your area. Obviously if you are landed with a complete clown – which happens – then you must call a meeting and sort your differences out or look for another PH. I once had an elk-hunting guide who was hopeless. On our second day of hunting, he got us lost and, after an argument, I went my own way and I found my way back to the truck, with him arriving more than an hour later!

But you should know and trust your PH way before you arrive for your hunt. Be sure to know all the ins and outs, from deposits to secure the hunt, to prices, to meet and greet, to weapons import, to dip and pack and shipment of trophies, to tips for your PH and camp staff. Be sure to go through it all and know what is expected from you. Tips for example – I have had clients giving too much and forking out $100 notes every day and all it did was turn my hunting staff and trackers into a drunken bunch of louts.

Then I have had clients leaving a waiter $20 for a 14-day leopard hunt! This was the guy who gave him a wake-up call with hot coffee at 4.30 a.m. every day! The same waiter worked till midnight tidying up the dinner hall and remains and then was up at 3.30 to make a fire and some nice hot water for his hunter. I hope that guy does not come back.

My point is, we only want it to be fair, and tipping is a massive part of a safari. The PHs and guys on the ground do not make huge amounts of money and their tips have become an important and integral part of their annual income. Without them, your safari is completely pointless. The agent and outfitter only send you there. These guys are the real deal and the guys that make things happen for you. Please discuss it with your PH – he will know the correct way of handling things. Ask about where you are hunting. A duffel bag full of exercise books, pens, pencils, erasers and other school stuff will go a hell of a long way at the local community school, or a bag of medical supplies to the local clinic – this is the future for the survival of wildlife and we need to encourage it.

Trophies – this is a very important part of the hunt. I like a client to come with his own tags which have his name and address on one side and his taxidermist's name and address on the other. Have them laminated and bring a bunch! Every time you shoot an animal, be sure to be very specific of what type of mount you want the skinners to do. Once they have skinned and processed the animal, be sure to check it and see for yourself that it is well covered in the salt pile.

THANK YOU

In closing, I want to thank you all for making it this far through my little book! I hope it has helped in some way and I hope that it will better your experiences in Southern Africa and hope it will make you a better hunter! My contact details are at the end of this book – please feel free and do not hesitate to contact me if you have any questions or if I can be of any help to anyone at all.

Please folks, bear in mind that without hunting and sustainable wildlife use (culling for meat, live sales and hunting) there is no future for wildlife. If there was no value for beef or chicken we as humans would have eradicated them to make space for something else. It is a shrinking world, and space for human livelihoods is far more in demand than the protection of animals and their habitat. Help us as hunters to educate as many people as possible - women, men, and kids alike - about the importance of hunting and sustainable use. Our children of today are losing touch with the great outdoors. Make a point of encouraging it with your kids and any other kids you can. It is an experience that makes them better people and teaches them to respect life. They are our future. They are the future of wildlife.

Please help us to do this all the while being an ethical bowhunter. Many people are quicker to accept a bowhunter as opposed to the rifle hunter. This is because we are closer to our roots and using our instincts and giving the animal a fairer chance. Just make sure your shot is good and the kill clean, and make us all proud.

In closing I want to thank some people who have impacted on my life as a hunter.

My parents for raising me right.

My wife and kids for putting up with me being away
hunting - a lot! It means the world to me.

My friends for making hunting fun.

And finally, my clients past and present for all their
support and for giving me the experience I have today.

THANK YOU.

Strang Middleton 260 977 826889 – text and WhatsApp
strangm76@gmail.com

STRANG MIDDLETON
S A F A R I S

NOTES